Let Her Fly

A Father's Journey
and the Fight for Equality

Exclusive Signed Edition

WH
ALLEN

Let Her Fly

Let Her Fly

A Father's Journey
and the Fight for Equality

ZIAUDDIN YOUSAFZAI
With LOUISE CARPENTER

1 3 5 7 9 10 8 6 4 2

WH Allen, an imprint of Ebury Publishing,
20 Vauxhall Bridge Road,
London SW1V 2SA

WH Allen is part of the Penguin Random House group of companies
whose addresses can be found at global.penguinrandomhouse.com

Copyright © Ziauddin Yousafzai 2018
Foreword copyright © Malala Yousafzai 2018

Ziauddin Yousafzai has asserted his right to be identified as
the author of this Work in accordance with the Copyright,
Designs and Patents Act 1988

First published in the United Kingdom by WH Allen in 2018
First published in the United States by Little, Brown and
Company in 2018

www.penguin.co.uk

A CIP catalogue record for this book is available from the British Library

Hardback ISBN 9780753552964
Trade Paperback ISBN 9780753552971

Printed and bound in Great Britain by Clays Ltd, Elcograf S.p.A.

Penguin Random House is committed to a sustainable future
for our business, our readers and our planet. This book is
made from Forest Stewardship Council® certified paper.

Contents

To Dr. Col. Muhammad Junaid and Dr. Mumtaz Ali, who performed lifesaving surgery on Malala in Pakistan after she was shot. With the grace of God, they saved Malala's life.

Let Her Fly

Foreword

By Malala Yousafzai

I WRITE THIS FOREWORD to thank my father.

For as long as I have known him, my father has been the personification of love, compassion, and humility. He taught me about love, not simply through words, but through his own acts of love and kindness. I never saw my father being disrespectful or unfair to anyone. Everyone was equal to him, whether Muslim or Christian, fair or dark, poor or rich, man or woman. As a school principal, a social activist, an active social worker, he was caring, respectful, and supportive to everyone. Everyone loved him. He became my idol.

We were not a rich family financially, but we were ethically and morally rich. Aba has the view that for a happy life wealth is neither a factor nor a safeguard. We never ever felt poor, though I precisely remember those times when we did not have enough money for food. If my father made a little money from school profits, he would spend most of it in one day on the family, buying fruit, and would give the rest to my mum, as she was the one sorting out the family's shopping for furniture, cutlery, etc. Shopping was boring for him, so boring that he would often start arguing with my mum if she took too long. My mum would tell him off and remind him, "You will thank me when you wear this suit." He loved seeing my brothers, my mum, and me happy and healthy. For him we had what mattered most in our lives: education, respect, and unconditional love, which was enough to make us feel rich and happy.

His love for me made him my shield from all things bad and evil around me. I grew up to be a happy, confident child, even in a society that was not offering the happiest outlook for my future as a woman. A deep respect for women and girls filled the home I grew up in, even when it was not mirrored in the world beyond our walls. But my father provided me with the shield of love. He was my defense in a society that did not treat me as equal. From the beginning, he stood against everything that threatened my future. Equality was my right, and he made sure that I got it.

This culture of respect in our home, especially for women, came with Aba's belief in the value of living life to the fullest and taking the chances that it gives us. I learned from him that I must do the best I can, that I must be the best I can be, and that I should respect people no matter where they come from.

My father and I have been friends since the very beginning and still are, which becomes rare as girls grow older and a gap starts developing. I used to share almost everything with my dad, more than I would with my mum, from complaining about period pain to asking him to get me period pads. In fact, I was quite scared of my mum, as she was strict. My father would always take my side if I got into an argument with my brothers—which would kind of happen every day!

I was not any different from the other girls in my class in Pakistan, my friends from my neighborhood, and the other girls of the Swat Valley. But I had the invaluable opportunity of receiving a supportive and encouraging upbringing. It was not that my father would give long lectures or advice to me every day. It was rather that his manners, his dedication to social change, his honesty, his openness, his vision, and his behavior had a big influence on me. I was constantly appreciated by my dad. I was always being told "You are doing so well in your studies, Jani," "You are speaking so well." *Jani*, which means "love" or "soul mate," is his nickname for me. I was always recognized and encouraged for my little accomplishments, my schoolwork, art, speaking competitions, everything. My dad was always proud of me. He believed in me more than I believed in myself. And this gave me confidence that I could do anything and everything.

My father is a great listener, and this is one of his qualities that I have always loved. Of course, I am exempting the times when he is busy on his iPad on Twitter. Then you have to call his name, "Aba," at least ten times for him to respond. Though he says "Yes, Jani," every time I call him, he is actually not listening while he is on Twitter, and I can tell. When he is listening to people, especially children, he is fully engaged and completely attentive to what they have to say. He was like that with me as well. He always listened to me, to my little stories, my complaints, my worries, and all my plans. My father made me realize that my voice was powerful and that it was important. This is what encouraged me to use my voice and gave me immense confidence. I knew how to tell a story, I knew how to speak up, and when the Taliban came, I felt I had the power to raise my voice to defend my education and my rights.

Growing up, I began to see how different my parents were when girls around me were either stopped from going to school or were not allowed to go to places where the crowd included men and boys. We lose so many women and girls in this kind of society, where men decide how women should live and what women should do. I have seen incredible girls who were forced to give up their education and their futures. These girls were never given a chance to be themselves. But I was not one of those girls. I would give speeches in places where only boys were speaking, and all around me I'd hear men saying, "These girls should be kept separate!" Some of my own classmates and friends were forbidden by their fathers and brothers from taking part in these school debates between girls and boys. My father was strongly against this mind-set and wanted it to change.

I remember that my dad would be in the guest room of our house with his friends and elder men visiting him, having a conversation, and I would take tea in for them and sit down and join them. My dad never said, "Malala, you know, we are having an adult conversation here, discussing politics." He would let me sit and listen, and, more than that, he would let me tell the room my opinion.

This is important because a girl growing up in an unequal home or society has to fight her fears that her dreams for herself will not come true. For millions of girls, school is a safer place than home. At home, they are told to cook and clean and prepare for marriage. Even for me, with my parents, school represented safety from society's limitations. When I went to school, my world was my amazing teachers and my amazing principal, and beside me in the classroom were my friends, and we were all talking about learning and our dreams for our futures.

It is hard to express just how much I loved going to the school that my father started. When I was learning, I could almost feel my brain physically growing bigger and bigger. I knew it was the information that was expanding my mind, all the different things that were filling my head, broadening my horizon.

The dad who brought me up is still the same today. He is idealistic. In addition to being a schoolteacher, he is also a poet. Sometimes I think he lives in a world of romance, a world of love for people, a world of love for his friends, his family, and for all human beings. I don't like reading poetry, but I do get this message of love.

People who want change in our world often give up too early or they don't even start. They say, "It's a big issue. What can I do? How can I help?" But my dad always believed in himself, and in his power to bring even the smallest change. He taught me that even if you can help only one person, you should not feel this is a small contribution. Every little bit of help counts in the grand scheme of things. Success, for my dad, is not only about reaching a goal. There is beauty in starting the journey, being on the journey, contributing to and encouraging change.

My father might not be able to convince the whole world to treat women with respect and equality, which he is still trying to do every day, but he did change my life for the better. He gave me a future, he gave me my voice, and he let me fly!

Aba, how can I ever thank you?

Prologue

So MANY PEOPLE ask me, with love and kindness in their hearts, "What has been your proudest moment, Ziauddin?" I think, perhaps, they are inviting me to reply, "Of course, it was when Malala received the Nobel Peace Prize!" or "When she spoke to the UN in New York for the first time" or "When she met the queen."

Malala is honored and respected around the world, but this question is impossible for me to answer because at its heart it is a question that is not really about Malala my child but about how influential she has been. Is her talking to a queen or a head of state more deserving of my pride than a Peace Prize? This is impossible for me to say.

What I say to this question instead is, "Malala makes me proud every single day," and I say that with absolute honesty. My Malala is as much the girl who makes me laugh at the breakfast table with her dry wit, so much sharper than my own, as the girl who for a great deal of her life went to a simple street school in Mingora, Pakistan, and yet proved herself stronger than the Taliban.

I have never met another child so in love with learning. And while the world might think, "Oh, Malala, she is so clever!" like many students, she sometimes struggles with the workload. As a cold English day fades to an even colder English night—and we Yousafzais, so used to the sun's rays burning into our skin, feel the English chill through to the marrow of our bones—Malala is often up in her bedroom, a lamp shining down on her textbooks, her brow furrowed. And she is working, studying, always studying, worrying about her grades.

The blessing of Malala's life—her "second life," as her mother, Toor Pekai, has called it since God saved Malala from the attack that she suffered—is not only that Malala has dedicated it to furthering the rights of *all* girls. It is also that Malala herself gets to live her *own* dream. Sometimes, for a parent, a moment of true beauty, of luck, of love, of marveling, *How can this extraordinary child be mine?!* finds its home in the seemingly most inconsequential of things: a look in the eye, a gesture, a beautiful comment, wise and yet innocent. So if I am to be pressed for my proudest moment so far in being Malala's father I will tell you that it involved Oxford University and the making and taking of a simple cup of tea.

Since we moved to Britain, Malala had always been very clear that she wanted to read Politics, Philosophy, and Economics at Oxford University. It was a choice that was also made by Benazir Bhutto, our country's first female prime minister.

Malala was not new to Oxford University, which of course is famous all over the world. Her public campaign had meant that she had delivered speeches there three or four times since we moved to Birmingham, and each time I had accompanied her. By then, she was old enough to look after herself, and there was no longer any need for me to iron her brightly colored shalwar kamiz and scarves, chosen for her by her mother, or polish her shoes as I had done when we were on the road with the campaign for girls' education in Pakistan.

I loved carrying out these so-called chores for Malala and I miss them now that she is fully independent. Why did I love meeting these domestic needs so much? Because in these small acts I felt I was able to express love and support for my child, and for her gender. It was the same sentiment that had propelled me after her birth—my blessed girl child—to include her name, the first female name for three hundred years, on our ancient family tree. It was a way of showing the world, showing myself, not only in words but in actions that girls are equal to boys; they matter, their needs matter; even the smallest ones like having a clean pair of shoes.

I understand that these small acts of servitude are carried out quite naturally by mothers and fathers all over the world for their children, girls and boys, in many different cultures, but for me, as a middle-aged man from a patriarchal society in Pakistan, it has been a journey.

I come from a land where women have served me all my life. I come from a family in which my gender made me special. But I did not want to be special for this reason.

When I was a child, growing up in Shangla, the long hot days were punctuated for us men and boys by refreshments, prepared and served to us for our comfort. They were then cleared away. We did not have to even click our fingers or nod our heads. It was a routine with deep winding roots across hundreds of years of patriarchy, unconscious, unspoken, natural.

I never once saw my father or my brother approach the stove in our basic family home, built of mud. During my childhood,

I never went near the stove, either. Cooking was not for me, or any man. As a child I accepted this truth unchallenged.

The smell of the cooking curry would always be accompanied by the fast and animated chatter of my mother and my sisters, gossiping as they chopped and diced, instinctively knowing that the juicy bits of the chicken they were preparing, the legs, the breast, would not pass their own lips but would be served to me—their younger brother, a child—to their older brother, and to their father. These accomplished female cooks of my family, hot from the stove and the steam and the slaving, would make do with the bonier parts.

Their eagerness to serve us, to make us feel comfortable, was also clear in their making of tea, which took an even greater part in the rhythm of our days. In my opinion, the tea we drink in Pakistan is the most delicious in the world. It is hot and sweet and milky, and now that I live in England, I can say that it is nothing like the world-famous English tea, which I will admit I cannot drink.

Like so many parts of my old world, tea in Pakistan is the product of ritual. First, the pot must be completely clean, with no residue from previous tea-making. Then the tea leaves must be of good quality. The pot is then filled with water, which is boiled up with the tea leaves. When this boiling is fierce, milk is added and then sugar. It is then reheated. At this point, a woman will take a ladle and bring it in and out of the pan, filling the cupped end with liquid, raising it up from the pan and then pouring it down again into the mixture. I still do not understand why this happens, but the women of my house always made tea in this way and our tea was hot and sweet and delicious. There is an even stronger variation, too, doodh pati, where no water is used at all and instead a larger quantity of milk is boiled first, with tea leaves and sugar added next, and then reheated until it is like liquid honey.

We menfolk never made this delicious tea; we simply enjoyed it. One of my earliest memories is as a young boy sitting in our small living room, with my father lounging on a cot bed, propped up with cushions. My mother entered the room carrying a tray, a pot, and two cups. My father did not look up from what he was reading, probably a heavy volume of hadith, a collection of traditions containing sayings of the Prophet Muhammad (PBUH). She pulled up a table, placed the tray down on it, and poured the hot sweet tea into a cup. She handed it to him and then poured a second for me, her small cherished son, to enjoy. And then she waited.

She waited to ensure that my father and I had drunk all that we required before taking her own refreshment. Sometimes my father would express gratitude, but not always.

The quality of tea you are given can be judged in three stages, he told me. First, a man must look at the tea as it is poured down from kettle to cup, observing the texture. Next, he said, observe the color of the tea in the cup. And then finally, he said, the ultimate test is when you take it to your lips.

For many years, all my father, uncles, and I had to do to enjoy a cup of tea was lift the cup to our lips. If my father found fault with it, he would not have known how to make a cup for himself. My mother or sisters would simply have been asked to go back to the kitchen to make it again. This rarely happened because my mother was an expert at knowing what pleased my father. It was, after all, her role in life to serve him.

*   *   *

On occasions of public speaking or debate, Malala has never seemed nervous. She rarely gets nervous anywhere, or overcome with emotion like me, except when she is around her teachers. I have seen her address the leaders of the Commonwealth with an almost supernatural calm and yet sitting beside me at the Parents Evening of Edgbaston High School, where she studied for her A levels, there would always be a small, almost imperceptible blush.

This same pink blush on her cheeks was there in August 2017, when four out of five of our family visited Lady Margaret Hall, at Oxford. We were elated and excited, having received the news that Malala had achieved her required grades and was able to take up her place at LMH eight weeks later.

Malala was nervous, I could tell. It was the first time Toor Pekai, her brother Khushal, and I had seen Lady Margaret Hall, with its imposing redbrick facade and its row upon row of arched windows. The beauty of Oxford University never ceases to fill me with awe. Nothing had prepared us for this, no former visits, no special Student Union speaker status. This time, Malala was simply the student and I was simply her father.

Two students gave us a tour, which Toor Pekai and I welcomed: the library was vast, with its high shelving containing book after book. The quantity alone was overwhelming. As a teacher, I have dedicated eighteen years of my life to learning and to helping others learn; how could I not feel emotional over these books? The Taliban had burned hundreds of schools, with books, and banned girls' education. It had threatened my life with words and almost taken my daughter's life with bullets, for being a girl who wanted to learn, to read. Look at us now; this was God's plan. Man proposes, God disposes. Malala had not only survived being shot for wanting an education, but she had shown the resilience to recover, heal, and continue to learn so that she could now be admitted to study at Oxford. I am an emotional man. Seeing my daughter about to fulfill her dream to study for a degree was overwhelming. "But Ziauddin," I told myself, "hold on to your tears for now."

After the tour, the principal of the college led us into a large drawing room with high ceilings; there was so much space and air for learning. I could feel the horizons widening within the four walls. Small clusters of people gathered around chairs and sofas, chatting in low voices. The motto of LMH is *Souvent me Souviens:* I often remember.

Across the room, I saw the principal make his way over to the tea-making machine. What would my father have made of such an invention? The principal picked up a cup, dropped in a tea bag from a nearby container, and placed the cup under the machine, filling the cup with hot water. After a few seconds, he placed the cup on a saucer and poured in some milk. After stirring the tea and throwing out the tea bag, he picked up the cup and saucer and crossed the room with this one cup of tea. There were lots of us who did not have a cup to hold, but he continued until he reached his destination and at that point, he handed the cup to Malala.

Souvent me Souviens. Only then I started to cry.

And so if you ask me now, "Ziauddin, what is your proudest moment to date?" I will say to you, it was when the male principal of Lady Margaret Hall made and served Malala a cup of tea. It was a moment so natural, so normal, and therefore more beautiful and powerful for me than any audience Malala might have had with a king or a queen or a president. It proved what I have believed for so long: when you stand for a change, that change comes.

This cup of tea was brewed in a Western way so alien to us. My father would have refused to drink the kind of tea being handed to Malala. My father would have dismissed it, and a female member of the family would have quickly lifted it out of his hands and carried it away, chastened that he had been disappointed. But this moment of tea-taking was made all the sweeter for the fact that had my father been with us in that high and grand room, the cup would not have been his to reject. The cup would have passed him by on its route towards his granddaughter.

As a child, I grew up believing society's patriarchal ideas. Only in my teenage years did I begin to question everything I had taken for granted. This is what my life has felt like: reaching towards something else, finding it, and learning it from scratch. What was this thing I yearned for long before Malala was born? And then wanted for her, and for my own wife, and then for my girl students, and then for all girls and all women on God's beautiful earth? I did not articulate it, initially, as feminism. This is a valuable label that I would later learn in the West, but I was unaware of feminism then. For more than forty years, I had no idea what it meant. When it was explained to me, I said, "Oh, I have been a feminist for most of my life, almost from the beginning!" While living in Pakistan, I saw my own shifting ideas to be based more on love, decency, and humanity. I simply wanted, and continue to want, for girls everywhere to live in a world that treats them with love and meets them with open arms. I wanted then and still want the end of patriarchy, of a man-made system of ideas that thrives on fear, that dresses up suppression and hatred as the tenets of religion, and that at its heart fails to understand the beauty to be had for us all in living in a truly equal society.

This is why I shed my tears over a simple cup of tea, because it symbolized the end of a fight I had waged for two decades to ensure equality for Malala. Malala is an adult now, old enough, and experienced enough, and brave enough to fight her own fight. But the fight for all girls, all over the world, is not yet over. All girls, all women, deserve the respect men have automatically. All girls should be offered a cup of tea in their learned institution—be it in Pakistan, in Nigeria, in India, in America, in the UK—both for its own sake, and for all that it symbolizes.

The road towards experiencing the kind of deep love and joy I feel when I see that my daughter is truly equal is not always an easy one for those of us who have been brought up in patriarchal societies. In learning these new ways of life, I had to unlearn all that came before. The first person I came across blocking my way was far more dangerous to me than any ancient Pashtun warrior with shield and dagger. It was me, my old self, the old Ziauddin, whispering in my ear, "Where are you going? Turn back! Do not be so foolish. It's cold and lonely on this path and everything you need to feel comfortable is back from where you came."

It has been a journey, a traumatic one not without sacrifice; I almost lost the very person for whom I began the fight. But Malala is alive and educated. I am alive, her mother is alive, her brothers are alive, and in so many different ways, we are all being educated, Malala and her brothers by books, their mother, Toor Pekai, too. I hope I continue to learn lessons from life itself, with all its rewards and disappointments, its deep joys and its many challenges.

I have written this book in the hope that one day it might provide some support and encouragement to women, girls, men, and boys everywhere who are courageous enough to demand equality, just as our family does.

For only when a girl like Malala, from the soil and the mountains, is handed a cup of tea by the principal of a college in a once patriarchal society, only when through a quality education does she grow up to be that principal herself, only then will our work be done.

Father

OUR AUTUMN HOUSE

WHEN I WAS barely old enough to write my name, with a pen fashioned from bamboo and ink drained from a carbon battery, my mother crept to my cot bed early one morning full of hope and purpose: "Ziauddin," she whispered, "wake up!" The room in our mud house was full of my sleeping sisters.

"Beybey?" I asked her, our word for "mama."

"Ziauddin, wake up!" she repeated. "We are going on a journey." I could see she was already dressed in her thick gray *paroonay.* "With School Kaka?" I asked her sleepily, about my father. "With School Kaka?" I repeated. "No," she said, "not with School Kaka. Your father is taking daily prayers, as usual, and teaching in the school. Fazli Hakeem, your father's cousin, will come with us. We are going up Shalmano Mountain. You must try to be strong because it is a long walk to the top, but it will be worth it because when we get there, it will help you achieve your dreams."

I did not know what my dreams were, but I knew that my mother and my father had big ones for me. And I knew they did not have them for anybody else. If Beybey and School Kaka thought something was at the top of that mountain, then I wanted to go up there.

Every morning in Barkana, our village deep in the Shangla district of northern Pakistan, the cocks would crow outside our house and our two buffaloes in the fields a mile away would stir in anticipation of my brother's bucket of feed. My brother's principal role in life was to feed and fatten these creatures, and to support my father and the family further. My brother seemed so happy, cultivating these prized female creatures and following my father in his own simple life: "When a man is happy, his wife gives birth to boy children and his buffalo gives birth to a female," my father would say. This was particularly bad for my poor mother, very bad. In our small muddy house there were nine of us in two rooms. My brother moved later to an add-on room behind with his new bride. The buffaloes he tended did not always have girl buffaloes. My father would meticulously log their issues in a book, which he kept with his diaries and journals on a shelf in the house.

My mother bore my father's children seven times and she provided a prized boy child only twice. The first time was with my brother, and then again with me. In between us, there were three daughters, and there would be two more to come. Their names are Hameeda Bano, Najma Bibi, Bakhti Mahal, Gul Raina, and Naseem Akhtar. I name them here because during my childhood I never once saw their names written down. They were described only in relation to men: daughters of my father, sisters of Ziauddin and Saeed Ramzan. They were never named in their own right. It was the same when I saw my mother described: wife of Rohul Amin, mother of Ziauddin or Saeed Ramzan.

That our family was weighted towards females was made worse by the boy-heavy family in the mud house next door.

Our cousins—my uncle's family—lived there, with its mud roof laid on top, just like ours. The roofs formed a sort of small rooftop playground, called a *chum*, where we young children would play our games, boys and girls together, shouting and hopping and rolling our marbles. My girl playmates were the preadolescent females of Barkana, carefree and careless, not yet considered old enough to invite shame or challenge honor. These same little girls in playful games of mimicry would some-times drape their mothers' or older sisters' shawls over their faces, covering their small noses and soft cheeks, obscuring all but their eyes, wanting to be just like these female role models whom they loved. Within a few years, when my playmates were around the age of twelve or thirteen, the shawls would become theirs to wear all the time. The need to protect their honor in their adolescence would pull them down off their rooftop play-grounds and away from the streets where they had once run from house to house, to live in purdah within four muddy walls. Once above, now below, my former playmates—my younger sisters, too—could hear the thumping childish feet on the roof above them, a reminder of their past freedom. I and the rest of the boys would carry on playing cricket. As I grew up, girls fell away from sight like this, like bright stars falling from the sky, and I never once questioned it. They would be under my feet, cooking and gossiping, and within a few years they would be married and pregnant, or if still single, heavy with dread at the prospect of being married off.

My mother took great care of the mud walls of our house. Once a year, she would spread new fresh mud over the insides of them, smoothing and re-smoothing as she went, with as much pride and patience as one restoring the finest walls of the finest grand house. But my mother's attention to the walls that confined her and my sisters could not stop my uncle's good fortune seeping through. As my male cousins kept arriving, the women of the village congregating around my aunt, offering their congratulations, my father's frustration would deepen at his misfortune in fathering so many daughters. "Why is there always spring in their house and autumn in ours?" he would ask.

We Pashtuns are a feuding race. Sons mean a man has an army. Fights, usually verbal, and conflicts were frequent. If fathers fought with their brothers, the sons of these men fought and competed, too. If uncles were at war, cousins followed. We two boys were not enough in terms of our father's army. My sisters were no resource at all. There were a few things that put my father in a bad mood. Jealousy was one of them.

"You will never be happy in your life," my mother once said to him as we all watched openmouthed in astonishment. "When you are in paradise, you will say, 'Oh, the next-door paradise is better.'"

My father regularly moaned about the good fortune of our cousins. Years later, when I had left his home both spiritually and geographically, he said, "Why has my nephew got a car? Why have not my own sons got a car? Why have I been failed by my boys in this way?" Cars had been in our village for some while by the time this happened and he had never once expressed envy about them. I—much older by then—said to him, "School Kaka, be pleased. You will never have to walk home again. When your nephew sees you on the road, he will be obliged to stop and give you a lift. You will never again have to travel on foot because it is your position as an elder to be given a lift." I was trying to make him see that there were benefits for him in his nephew's good fortune. It was poor consolation. He did not want a lift in his *nephew's* car.

How I hated these jealousies, hated them! And the corrosive power they had to eat away at love and happiness. But if these feudal jealousies pained me, it was nothing to the injustice of my sisters' lives compared with my own.

I occupied a unique position in the family. From a very young age, both my father and my mother talked of me as being something different, a child who could soar above our fairly low social status, fulfilling expectations never once placed on any of my sisters and not even my brother before me. They said they had spotted in me a spark, which invited the possibility of a better life, the climbing up towards a new social class. The ladder was education. Had they looked for this spark in my sisters, I am sure they would have seen it there. But they did not look for it.

I understand what they mean about this spark in a child, because I saw the same thing in Malala when she was small. It is a quality that marks the child as different, an intensity, perhaps. At the very least it is a child who invites you—allows you—to encourage them to greatness. Why was it that they had these dreams for me and not my brother? I think perhaps it is because he wanted a simple life. Every night, my father laid out three almonds. "Ziauddin, please eat these nuts." They were to improve my brain. I ate them readily. Another privilege.

If we ever journeyed beyond Barkana, my mother would point to the fine bungalows, which, compared with our mud hut, seemed like palaces to me. "Who lives there, Beybey?" I would ask her, my small hand threaded through hers. I, a small boy child barely up to her waist, was her chaperone rather than she mine. And my mother would say as we moved through the street, "Ziauddin, educated people live there. If you work hard, you can live there, too." We were not feudal lords, or people of business or industry. My parents understood that if they were to propel me to this better life, it would have to be through education. We had no money. We had no connections. We had no industry. Education was my only chance.

At the start of each day, my father, brother, and I were given the cream from the milk. At the day's close, the juiciest parts of the chicken would be ours, too. My mother liked to make my father his favorite omelet, flavoring it with diced cucumbers and tomatoes gathered from the fields. She mixed the eggs up with cream from the milk. When it came to eating our food, my mother and my sisters were not at our table. They ate in another room. My sisters' shoes were patched, frayed, and often falling apart, but mine were new, their leather straps strong and firm against my feet.

Only once did I ever hear a sister complain. Najma Bibi, one of my older sisters, said to my mother, "If you are so fond of boys, why did you have us?" And my mother replied, "It was not in my power. I could not help it." My mother seemed angry, and I saw a sort of confusion in my sister's face, too.

My father was a maulana (religious scholar) in our village, leading prayers five times a day in Barkana's lower mosque, also made of mud, as opposed to its bigger, higher mosque, to which I would later gravitate. He was also a teacher of boys in the next village.

The relatively low status of being a religious cleric contributed to his sometimes unpredictable temper and anxiety about money. While his clearly defined religious role placed him outside the caste system and brought a degree of respect, it had a stigma attached to it, the unspoken but acknowledged truth that my father needed the job because he needed the money.

Maulanas receive a stipend from the community they serve for the role they perform. My father did not need to be a maulana even though he was well qualified to be one. He was already a theology teacher in a public school, but he led prayers to boost his income.

Fear of my father's temper jostled with my deep love for him. He shouted about small things, like lost chickens or spilled grain, and these outbursts were never predictable. But I was never in any doubt that my father loved me. He loved me so much—this I knew. He would take me into his lap and lull me in such a gentle way. When I was a small child, his hair was still black, but hair and beard both were flecked with age, hints of the later whiteness that would form my resounding memory of him: my father the maulana, the teacher, the orator, in his long white robes, with his white hair and white beard, white skullcap or a white turban for Friday prayers. He gave me so much of his time and his energy. He was always reading to me and trying to enrich my mind. It was he who instilled in me a lifelong love of learning.

My father was eloquent and passionate, so that when he preached the villagers began recording him so they could listen to him in their homes.

Eleven years after my father's death, I love and respect his departed soul with as much intensity as I did when I was in his lap or listening to him read me Iqbal and Saadi, I his golden child, the focus of all his patriarchal hopes and dreams. My love for him is unconditional. Just as I was to go on a long journey with my mother up a mountain, my father, decades later, would go on a journey, too, one that began with Malala's birth and was to bring him much closer to me—to all of us—by the time of his death.

"UNTIE THE KNOT OF MY TONGUE"

There was a reason why it was me accompanying my mother and Fazli Hakeem up the mountain and not my sisters. For once in our lives, it had nothing to do with the patriarchy that ruled our house. My sisters had one huge advantage over my brother and me. My father might have disfavored them in every way, but nature had compensated. My five sisters all had flowing tongues, whereas both my brother and I had developed a stammer around the age of four. I do not know if my brother had been encouraged to overcome his speech impediment. For me, it was important to my parents that this imperfection be mastered. How could I be a rich doctor if my words clogged my mouth, refusing to fly off my tongue?

Stammering is thought to be partly genetic, partly psychological. Boys develop stammers more than girls. In our case, one each of my maternal and paternal uncles were stammerers. Perhaps my sisters were spared a speech impediment because they were girls. Perhaps it was nature that had given my brother and me a stammer. But also, there was an environment where our stammer thrived. Our father took notice of us, of what we had to say, and so therefore he took notice, too, of what we could not say. We were boys so all eyes were on us. Nobody took notice of the girls with their perfect tongues. You could see our stammering as the only strike against the patriarchy in our home.

My father's unpredictable moods did not help my stammer. I was so desperate to impress him, to make him proud, but I was not a relaxed child in his presence.

Still, when I became stuck on words, choking and stuttering, he never once shouted, "Stop it, Ziauddin!" or "Get it out!" He did not blame me. He was not a cruel man. He was kind at heart. Perhaps this is why he sought help for me from a saint.

My mother and I and Fazli Hakeem began our journey by bus from Barkana. My mother told me we were going to Mian Kaley, a small village high up in the mountains to see the saint who lived there. "He will treat you for the stammering," my mother said softly. When he was younger, the saint had been very active in the communities, helping to build mosques and create pathways in the mountains. On such occasions, he would give blessings and there would always be more men beating sticks on drums, as an encouragement to the workers.

Mian Kaley was not accessible by bus, so after an hour's journey during which I suffered such terrible sickness, we got off the bus and began the walk up the mountain of Shalmano. The sun's rays were already beating down on us, and as we twisted and turned through the evergreens and sturdier-trunked trees than were on the flat parts where we lived, I quickly lost heart and wanted to stop. Fazli Hakeem pulled me onto his shoulders, and I wrapped my hands around the sides of his face, my fingertips resting under his chin. Tired from the early start, the traumatic bus ride, and the heat of the sun, I repeatedly nodded off, each time lunging forward so that Fazli Hakeem was forced to readjust to keep his footing.

"Ziauddin! Ziauddin! Wake up. Keep talking. Keep talking to me."

When we got to the top, my mother made her way to the saint's mud house, and as we drew closer there was a pungent smell of the mutton and rice that was cooked and distributed to visitors and the poor. The Holy Man, properly known as *Peer Sahib* or *Lewano Peer,* was a man of great generosity, this I knew. And I also knew that if you went to him and he prayed for you, your prayers and your wishes would be addressed by God.

After our meal of rice and mutton, my mother and I were led to him in a separate room. There were rooms for the women and rooms for the men, and I could see that this saint had at least three or four wives of his own.

He sat before me. I had never seen a man so old and so hairy. His hair was long and white but there was more white hair that seemed to sprout from other places, especially his ears. This scary ear hair was so long that in my child's eye I saw it flowing out of his lobes like a waterfall. He was also blind, and his long thin fingers seemed to feel around him with not much precision. "Ziauddin, the eyes of his heart are open," my mother whispered to me.

My mother must have already told him or a helper my problem. He murmured a few words from the Holy Quran and then he blew on me. He then pulled a ball of *gurr* from his pocket. It is a type of hardened sugar that we use in Pakistan. Rather than handing it to my mother as I expected, he put the sweet ball whole in his mouth. I watched him suck on it for a couple of seconds, and then he cupped his hand under his hairy mouth and spat it out. I was horrified to see that he handed this wet slippery ball to my mother. She broke off a bit and gave it to me. I was revolted by the slimy fragment, despite the miracle it was supposed to contain, but I put it into my mouth and chewed and then swallowed it. The ball came home with us and each night the routine was repeated. Even though the ball hardened, I saw it always covered in the saint's saliva.

I wish I could say that this saint cured me, but my stammer got worse. When I went to school, my stammer felt like a curse. Given that my sisters and other girls went uneducated, it feels ungrateful to complain about the misery my stammer made my early education, but I was badly teased. The boys would mimic me.

The curse of the stammer was compounded by two other things. The first was that we were not rich and the second was that my father was a maulana. Pakistan is a country of caste systems, and forty years ago the teachers openly favored the rich boys, especially the sons of the tribal lords. This made me so sad. I was a clever boy who tried hard. I needed my education.

Boys made fun of my father's position, so that I, too, began to feel pinched by it. Through prayer, my father provided a service to the community. My father wanted more than this for me. He could have said to me, "Ziauddin! You will be a maulana like I am, learning Islamic education only in seminary." But he did not say this. My father was an intellectual, who had received his own education beyond Shangla, in Karachi and Delhi, depending on the kindness and charity of the local communities, moving around with his begging bowl for food, as all Islamic scholars did at that time. He wanted a modern education for me, which was a rare thing and for which I will always thank him. But this big dream for me was focused on only one outcome: that I would be a well-paid doctor, bringing wealth and status to our family. It was another aspect of our social setup.

"The world is an open book, Ziauddin," he would say. "It is there for learning."

The message was clear: If you want these big dreams for yourself, you need to acquire an education. To be a doctor was the pinnacle.

But the problem was, I was not doctor material.

When I heard the *azaan* (call to prayer) during the day, I preferred running to the village's higher mosque, with its surrounding trees and insects buzzing in and out of its walls and a spring running through its middle, than the lower mosque at the other end of the village, near the bazaar, where my father would be in a special place at the front. There were no stereo speakers carrying the *azaan* over the village rooftops like there are today. During my childhood, men shouted the *azaan* from a patch of grass or from an elevated rock.

Even though I had a bad speech impediment I was determined to become an orator like my father. Perhaps this was the spark, the strength of character, that my parents had seen. It is true I was defiant when faced with my own weakness. I was defiant when I saw the rich boys and how much special treatment they got from the teachers. If I am to sum up my father's key gift to me, it is this: he helped me turn my weakness into a strength.

As I moved through the school grades, it became clear that I was one of the abler students. The teachers could not ignore it. If the rich boys got the attention for their family name, I won my share through hard work. But I was still my father's stutterer-son.

After the almonds, I'd spent a period of time eating raisins, which my mother soaked in milk each night. Each morning, the raisins were fat and juicy with the liquid and they were so tasty.

When I was thirteen years old and had moved to become a student in the high school in the next village where my father taught, words still refused to fly off my tongue. But I announced to my father that I was going to enter a speaking competition.

My father did something very important: he did not forbid me. Far from it. He encouraged me. He believed in me, and with his support, I felt stronger. School life in Pakistan is full of speaking and recitation competitions. My father agreed to write a speech for me.

I would practice it alone, hour after hour, my stammer mysteriously gone. But when I practiced it in my father's company, the same stutterer-son was back.

My father showed such patience. He might have lost his temper inside the house at petty things, but out in the world he was my patron. He stood beside me in support.

As an aid to my speaking, he taught me a famous prayer from the Holy Quran, which is the prayer of the Prophet Moses (AS), a stammerer, too, according to our holy book: "My Lord! Expand for me my breast [with assurance] and ease for me my task and untie the knot of my tongue that they may understand my speech" (Ta Ha 25–28).

Even today, with my stammer almost under control, I recite these lines before I am about to speak.

I delivered that first speech perfectly, in Urdu, our country's national language. I cannot say what happened, but it was exhilarating. Afterwards, my math teacher, Ahmed Kahn, approached me and said, "Shaheen, you spread the fire." *Shaheen* means falcon, and for a while my father said I should sign my name Shaheen. This success brought me closer to my father. It gave flight to his dreams for me, and it gave me confidence. I started to see myself in a different way, not as an ugly boy with dark skin and a big nose who had a stammer but as a boy who had come first in a debate and who could overcome weakness. I think confidence creates more confidence.

Competitions took place all over the region and we would travel everywhere together on the bus. On one occasion, I looked like a particularly poor candidate. On a long journey over the potholed roads, I suffered terrible travel sickness again. My face was pale and my skin was covered in sweat. Other contestants were also on the bus, and I could see that one of the boys' escort was looking at me with a kind of laughter. "You, will you be giving a speech?" I nodded. "No, you won't," he said, laughing. I could see I was joke to him. Nobody believed this sickly child would stand on the stage. But the next day, I beat not only that boy on the bus but the whole district. In that stammering tongue there was a great speaker. My success was the best answer to the escort's mockery. I call it positive revenge. It is a principle that underpins my whole life. It is a way of righting wrongs without hatred.

I wish I could say that this public eloquence was my stammer's cure. It was not. It would be many years before it got better in everyday life. It happened almost by accident, when I left Shangla to go to Swat to study science and English. It is still with me, but as I became older and was increasingly appreciated, my self-confidence grew and I was happier to accept that stammering was part of who I was. I met a very good doctor, a physiotherapist—I was never to be a doctor myself—who told me about Demosthenes, the Greek orator, and how he put pebbles under his tongue to cure his stammer. Demosthenes ran along the beach orating loudly over the sound of the waves. I used pebbles, too, and would roll words around my mouth in new exercises. But another part of my self-help was to choose different words from those I knew would get me stuck, so if I were to choose between "moon" and "sun," I'd choose "sun." If I knew I'd stammer on "woman," I instinctively chose "lady." It obstructed my fluency and sometimes I felt I did not have the best words under my control, but I was able to express my views. It was an equation: little word, more fluency, over stronger word and less fluency. It goes on even today.

When I was first asked to deliver an essay in front of the class at university and was tongue-tied yet again, my lecturer said, "Ziauddin, why don't you let somebody else read that for you?"

"I will be reading it myself," I told him. "By not letting me read it, you are taking away part of me." My lecturer's face was full of shame. He was horrified at his mistake. "You are quite right," he said. "Go ahead."

I read the piece of work. I was unable to switch the words around and I was slow and un-fluent, but I remember thinking, "This is me, this is who I am."

Years later my speech would become my weapon against the Taliban. I might not have been fluent, but I spoke the truth. During those years when the Taliban invaded our valley and took away our life, I encountered so much verbal fluency, so much rhetoric, but in those free-flowing, easy speeches made by the commanders over FM radio and over our squares, there were lies beneath. My own voice might have stopped and started, but it was not silent and it spoke the truth about how the Taliban wanted us to live in a country of darkness.

Ziauddin Yousafzai

THE LEGACY OF MY BEYBEY

My father might have instilled in me a love of education and a passion for oration, but it was my mother who provided unconditional kindness. In Islam, a man came to the Prophet Muhammad (PBUH) and said, "O Messenger of God! Who among the people is the most worthy of my good companionship?" The Prophet (PBUH) said, "Your mother."

The man said, "Then who?" The Prophet (PBUH) said, "Then your mother." The man asked further, "Then who?" The Prophet (PBUH) said, "Then your mother." The man asked again, "Then who?" The Prophet (PBUH) said, "Then your father."

These three mentions of "mother" remind me that when I published my first collection of Pashto poetry in 2000, I dedicated it to three women, all of whom were mothers to me in different ways—my first, real, mother; my second mother, who married my father after my mother died; and then my third "mother," a kind woman who treated me like a son while I boarded at her house during my college years.

My birth mother was called Shahrukh, abbreviated to Sharo, and I loved her so much and I still do even though she is in the next world. She was so caring to me. She was kind to all her children but to me especially because fairly early in my childhood my older brother got married and was then looked after by his wife.

You could say I was my mother's blue-eyed boy. Her stories about people in the neighborhood never stopped; how they were poor but still they were resilient; how they were hardworking; and of their struggles, too, through difficult times. And how despite their trials and tribulations, they were able to complete their education and to achieve a lot in their lives, to have good jobs, and if they were lucky, to become rich. I suppose you could say as a woman my mother gave me something beautiful. She was not educated herself, but she could see the value of education. She knew the only way I would live in a bungalow and enjoy the kind of life she did not have was through an education and a good job. Social norms meant she could not pass this knowledge on to her own daughters, but she could pass it on to me so that I, in turn, could hand it on to Malala.

My mother was beautiful, with off-white skin several shades lighter than my own. But she was not in strong health. When we went to the male doctor, he would write, "Mother of Ziauddin" or "Wife of Rohul Amin." Sometimes, the doctor would visit her at our house, and I used to hold his box, carrying his stethoscope and thermometer, for him. In my own way, I saw this as serving my mother, but it was no match for what she did for me.

By the time I was in the final year of high school in the next village, where my father taught, approaching my exams at the age of sixteen, I had moved to a room in a little guesthouse built onto the front of our house. I would study there late into the night, lying on my cot bed surrounded by my books, with a kerosene lantern beside me. Every few hours I would see a ghostly shape pass by the window. It was like a mirage, and I would think, "Is that Beybey or some kind of ghost?"

One night, she woke me from a slumber. She was speaking so fast. The lamp had tipped over on my pillow, its flame dangerously close to igniting the bed.

I wish I had been able to save her in the same way. On May 5, 1985, my mother died. I was sixteen. I was sitting outside our house on a small verandah with my sister and my mother. It was a stressful time because of my school exams, especially as I knew I would not get the grades I needed to become a doctor.

One of my elder sisters had come to stay with us, sleeping in the same room as my mother. I had not registered the significance of this, but I can see it now. As it got late, I lifted my mother into my arms. She was so frail, so light, and she could not walk. I carried her inside and she was laughing and joking with me, "Ziauddin, put me down! What are you doing? Where are you taking me?" I laid her in the bed of the small house and went to bed myself with my books and my lamp. The following morning, I heard my sisters wailing and screaming, "Oh, my Beybey—oh, my Bey, Bey-bey." Mourning seemed to be everywhere. I ran into the main room of our mud house and I saw my mother lying in her bed, just as I had left her, but she was dead. Nobody had expected my mother to die. That same day, my sisters cleansed my mother's body and she was buried. Only one sister, in Karachi, was missing. She arrived by bus three days later after a long journey. News of my mother's funeral was shouted out across the village by the men who called *azaan,* so that everybody could attend. I could hardly believe this latest funeral announcement was for the person I loved most in the whole world.

My father had been very grieved, but after a few months he was thinking of marrying another woman. This quick replacement of lost wives is so normal in our society that I did not even question it. Men in our society do not live alone. I understood that my father *needed* a woman to perform all the basic functions that would keep him alive. My brother set about trying to find him a new wife from the pool of available women nearby. He was not looking for beauty or connections but a woman who could serve him in the same ways my mother had: washing his clothes, making his food, and caring for his children. Wife was a role, and without it a house could not survive.

Despite my own grief, I did not think, "Oh, my mother is gone and now my father is remarrying." Instead I thought, "He needs a companion to survive. I will have a second mother."

It was settled. My father was to marry a middle-aged widow. Soon, she was occupying all the places and parts of our family life that had been my mother's. I missed my mother so much, but I did not want to celebrate my mother or remember her in front of my second mother because I did not want to hurt her. Before the marriage, a villager told my father, "You are going to marry another woman, but you must keep in mind one thing: never praise your old wife, your previous wife, in front of your new wife. The jealousy of the two wives of one husband has no match. Not even among cousins are the jealousies so strong! It is the worst jealousy in the world."

When it came to our two Eid holidays, little Eid and big Eid, I would go to the graveyard to visit my departed mother and I would never discuss it with my new mother. Why should I hurt my new mother, who was a living soul with feelings? If knowing my loss hurt her feelings and the telling of it didn't benefit me in any way, there was no point.

My second mother is still alive. When Malala was shot by the Taliban in October 2012, my second mother was at our home in Mingora. It was her prayers Toor Pekai wanted the most "because God is so respectful of the old, of the gray of hair."

From early on, my second mother said of Malala, "May you be the Benazir Bhutto of your age, but may your life be long."

The unequal lives of my sisters and my mother had a great impact on me over the years. But even as a ten-year-old, I remember I was beginning to really enjoy serving women in the village. I was too young at that point for it to have been a kind of protest, but I remember the pleasure I felt in helping them. These women were mothers who were illiterate and whose sons were away working in the Gulf states. When the sons sent their families letters, it was often the case that the person who missed them most could not read and enjoy their news. I do not know how I came to understand this at such a young age, but I began reading sons' letters to mothers, and after that, I acted as a scribe. I would write letters for the women, putting their thoughts and feelings on the page exactly as they wanted so that they could communicate directly with the sons whom they missed and cherished, just like my mother cherished me.

In Barkana, it was my own cousin's fate that actively contributed to my change. It showed me that inequality can mean brutal violence, too. I will call my cousin Noor Bibi to protect her identity, but this is not her real name. She is four years older than me and she is still in contact with me, living a new life now in another part of Pakistan. Like me, she lost her mother, but her loss came when she was two and a half years old, so that she had no memories of happiness with her mother to treasure. Her father found a new wife, but this woman was not kind or affectionate, so my cousin often imagined what her life might have been like had her mother still been alive. At fourteen, my cousin was married off to a family of a higher status. It was considered a good match, but the man was mentally unstable. On their wedding night, he was brutal with her, and this continued. My cousin wept a river of tears. Years later, the river of tears was still flowing. "Ziauddin, what will I do? What will I do?" By the time of my own mother's death, I had become a very romantic boy. Because of the poetry I read, I was already full of ideas of pure and eternal love, the kind that rushes over you and raises you up to the clouds.

My reaction to my cousin's dreadful reality was against this backdrop of my high ideals about love. I hated her distress. I could not bear the profound injustice of her life. Marriage, while always arranged with the involvement of families, still meant a life of love for me. I aspired to a loving union, but my cousin's marriage was shaped by disrespect and unhappiness.

When I was sixteen, my cousin was already twenty. She had tolerated a few months of marriage as a teenage bride and then run home to her father. When he died, she went to live with one of her brothers. Patriarchy forces women to become a burden, and this was the case with my cousin. She went from father to husband, back to father, and then to brother, with no means of supporting herself or living independently.

There began a process over years to free my cousin from the marriage that had been arranged for her. Her brother filed a petition in the courts for divorce, but the family was put under strong social pressure by the opposing family. The shame of this failed marriage ran deep and my cousin cried so much. I became among her closest friends, as there was nobody else to help her. Her struggle was to contribute to my change.

Failing to find any formal help, she recited special verses to God at midnight, holding her hands out to him and literally begging for mercy and salvation. I saw that our society was not built to protect her, that the law-enforcement agencies were not interested.

In desperation, my cousin also began visiting so-called miracle makers, cheaters, and con men who played tricks with her heart, promising to reverse her bad fortune.

"Ziauddin," she said to me one afternoon, "please come to the graveyard with me." Even as a teenage boy, I found the graveyard a frightening place, but my cousin had been given an amulet and had been told to find the oldest grave possible in which to bury it. Its metaphysical power would reverse her fortunes. She was desperate and hopeful, so I agreed. We went at midday. My cousin paced the graveyard as if she were almost mad. When she found an old grave, she began digging with her hands, chanting and praying.

Two years later my cousin was shot in the leg by an unknown assassin armed with a Kalashnikov. She was taken to the hospital with a 4 cm bullet wound to her leg and remained there for four and a half months before being released. Today, she still walks with a limp. I was eighteen and no longer living under my father's roof in Barkana when I began visiting her in the hospital. I was reading many new ideas and meeting more people, and as my ideas about life slowly began to inch away from the community in which I had grown up, I vowed that if I had a girl child, I would never let her endure the kind of life forced on my cousin. It took eight more years after my cousin was shot and two more unhappy marriages before she finally found happiness in her fourth marriage.

When I think of what Malala has achieved, I also think about the other women in my life whom I have loved, women like my cousin and my sisters, whom I could not protect from society's cruelty and unfairness. It took my witnessing the unfairness of their lives to vow that my own family would follow a different path These other women, Malala's aunts and second cousins and her grandmothers, spent their lives dreaming other people's dreams and obeying other people's wishes. I think of all the power they carried inside them. But that power was unexplored, undiscovered, underestimated. Nobody wanted to believe in it.

When the stories and the lives of people around us are like this, they bring a change in us. I began rethinking the cultural ideas of my father and his father and all the fathers in Pakistan before that.

A SONG OF LIBERATION

I was such an obedient boy. If my father raged about richer cousins or chastised my mother about something small, I never once made any public or open protest to him. Where I come from, a son obeys a father, whatever he says. But when the results of my exams became known when I was sixteen, shortly after my mother's death, it was very clear that I was not going to fulfill my father's dream of my becoming a doctor. He lost interest in my education.

I had secured for myself a place at Jehanzeb College, the best in Swat, but my father was only prepared to pay partly towards my living expenses. Jehanzeb College was many miles away, in Saidu Sharif, a twin town to Mingora. While the tuition was free, it was impossible to attend Jehanzeb College without moving from Barkana. We had no family near the college, and so where would I stay? My father had received his higher religious education like a traditional Talib, living in mosques, with all food and clothing provided for free by the community. He did not understand why he should have to pay for these things, especially as there seemed to be little chance that I would become a doctor. I wanted to leave Shangla, for all its beauty, to pursue a bigger life, to learn for learning's sake.

But to my father this was a waste of money. He had encouraged Ziauddin the Falcon with strong wings, but I would not fly in the direction he wanted. I remember so clearly wandering the mountains, my cheeks wet with tears. My future felt so desperate. It felt lost. I saw myself marshaling buffaloes and teaching nothing but the most basic facts to the boys who lived high in the mountains.

At the very point when all seemed to be lost a miracle occurred. I had begun helping out in the school in the mountain village of Sewoor, where my brother taught. It was considered a very unprestigious school because it was an hour and a half's climb up in the mountains from Barkana, and it was full of the sons of peasants. Teachers did not like working there and most had little respect for the students, whose families lived in poverty. "Let them stay illiterate," people often said. But my brother was committed, and I began helping out there. The school did not even have a building. They used the mosque instead. One of my aunts had married a man in this village, and while I was teaching at the school they happened to be visited by a relative of my sister's husband. He was called Nasir Pacha, and he lived with his wife, Bakht Mina Jajai, in a village called Spal Bandai, within a short distance of Jehanzeb College. Nasir Pacha was impressed with my teaching at the hilltop school. I had given up hope of attending Jehanzeb College, and while I had told him that I'd been offered a place, I had not revealed I needed help to take it up. To my utter astonishment he said, "Come and live with us." As the bus drove me away from Barkana towards that beautiful village, I felt like my life was opening up. It was truly a blessing from God because it meant freedom. It was freedom of thought, freedom to make my life my own. My student life was not easy, as I was poor, but it was intellectually rich and I became known as a powerful student speaker and advocate. Throughout my college education, I subsisted on tiny bits of money here and there, occasionally from my father, sometimes from my brother. I did not dwell on my father's lack of financial support. Sometimes I wept in frustration, but I accepted circumstances for what they were because I knew that my father could not help the way he was.

My father had such high ideals. He talked all the time of Gandhi and Iqbal, but once I went to college I began to see that the high ideals of his pronouncements were not always matched by his day-to-day life. I suppose once I moved away and my ideas started to re-form, I began to see that he was flawed. We are all flawed, but it is a powerful moment when you realize this about your parents. Still, I loved him no less for it. I know I have flaws, and my children are free to realize this and make their own corrections.

I draw from my experience a handful of conclusions about parents. The first is that it is human nature that we go through our lives keeping an account of the relationships we have, good and bad. Has this brother or sister been good to me? Has that friend supported me in a time of need? Was so-and-so there for me at a point when I needed them the most? And was I there for them in return? It's a kind of tit for tat in all relationships, and I think it is very human. When somebody treats us well, we try to repay it. When somebody lets us down, we remember it. Ideally, we should be good to all those people who are good to us. And ideally, if they are bad to us, we must try to respond with goodness. But I feel our relationships with our parents must sit beyond all this. To cast it in terms of obedience implies we have to do as they wish. I do not mean this, but I do think respect is important. If change in our parents is needed, then that change can be encouraged respect-fully and in a positive way. Respect is a matter of both respecting their views and doing your own thing. In my relationship with my late father, I will not take account and weigh the good and bad. I will always be kind to my father, and will always love him. Some-times it is hard to love somebody when they disappoint you, or make you weep tears of frustration. But by focusing on what my father gave me, rather than what he did not, I can see myself built on all the best parts of him.

In patriarchal societies, children as well as women are seen as possessions of their parents. This becomes a problem for chil-dren like me who do not want to be a possession. I wanted to find a different way, to be myself, to open new avenues and live a different life from the one my father wanted for me. But I did not want to reject him. What I did instead was try to make him proud by achieving the dreams I dreamed for myself. In the end, I hope I showed my father that I followed and fulfilled my own dreams in a way that could make him a hundred times prouder than if I'd simply followed a path laid out by him.

I have thought a lot about change. When you stand against state corruption, or against racism or dictatorships or brutal regimes like the Taliban, sometimes a sudden shout, a sudden cry, a sudden angry protest, is needed, like the powerful rallies of Martin Luther King Jr., the strong female voices of the #MeToo campaign, or Malala's voice in her campaign for girls' education. But at that time, for the social change I wanted in my life—to treat women as equal—I believed the most important change began with me.

Once I had made that change in my life, which became easier once I was living in Spal Bandai, where women seemed freer in their movements, I felt I could begin to invite others to join me by example rather than force. I think I knew instinctively that I'd change nothing if I went back to Barkana and challenged the community all of a sudden, if I stood in the muddy house where my sisters and cousins were still rinsing the rice and delivered long impassioned speeches on female emancipation and the hatefulness of the patriarchy. I never once thought of bringing a sudden social change to my community. I wanted a different life from that of my tribe—and ultimately for it as well—but I did not want to spark a revolution.

The change in me was not sudden, either, but gradual. The attack on my cousin was not the only act of violence against women I saw in my community. There was an honor killing in our village, in which a young girl was poisoned and strangled by the male members of her family for her love of an unchosen boy. When her mother sought comfort under her dead daughter's favorite tree, the men of the family cut down that tree, the strength of its trunk and branches too much a reminder of the girl's life and defiance. Can you imagine losing your daughter and then watching the only thing left that brought you solace be taken away, too?

Set against this, I was discovering love, through marriage and fatherhood.

My first memory of my wife, Toor Pekai, is around the age of sixteen. Her father was my uncle's best friend, and they lived in Karshat, a neighboring village to Barkana. I was not allowed to speak to Toor Pekai, but whenever she visited my uncle's home, I found her beautiful, with fine features and green eyes and pale skin, an attribute of beauty in Pashtuns. The attraction was mutual although she gave no hint of that then. That would have brought a great shame on her family as marriages were arranged by the elders, not set in motion by a potential bride and groom.

I still thought of myself as an ugly boy, but I was known in my village for being clever and hardworking. Pekai—everybody called her Pekai—told me later that she valued my education more than how I looked. At the age of six, she started and then left school, having sold her books for nine annas, which she used to buy some boiled sweets. She had been the only girl and missed her friends so much that she quickly left to join them. By the time she got to her teenage years, it was far too late to return. She flicked ink over her clothes to give the impression that she was still a student.

What Pekai felt she lacked—education—she found in me. What I felt I lacked—beauty—I found in her. Almost immediately after our marriage I was to discover that her beauty went way beyond the physical.

I remember one afternoon walking home, after lying in the fields with my books, seeing a large group of laughing girls approaching. It was like a shoal of beautiful multicolored fish coming towards me, their scarves covering them almost entirely. I instinctively knew that Pekai would be among them and my heart began to race. I was with the old man who helped my brother with the buffaloes. "Quick," I said to him. "Give me a mirror!" He handed me his snuff box and using the mirrored lid I smoothed down my hair. As she passed, Pekai lifted her eyes and greeted me. *"Pakhair raghlay,"* she said. I was in the skies. Such a greeting from girl to boy was risky. She told me years later that as they approached she had been saying to her friends, "I'm going to do it. I'm going to greet him," and that they had said, "No, no, Pekai. You must not. It is not honorable."

I think these small things in retrospect marked Pekai out as different even then, but within this there were constraints. Once, some time later, I sent her my picture and she sent it straight back. The message was clear: I'd overstepped a mark. She could not risk carrying around a boy's picture. Our mutual attraction had to be made clear in more subtle ways. I tutored her nephew, for example, and sometimes I would open his book and see Pekai had made a small note or mark. Who did that? I would ask him, and when he said, "Toor Pekai," my heart would thud in my chest. I knew she had wanted me to see it. Sometimes, feeling so desperate for not being able to talk to her, I would sit in the fields and talk to the stones, in a kind of pretense that it was she whom I could tell how deeply I felt about her.

Just before my mother's death, my mother saw in me this kind of lovesickness when it came to Toor Pekai. I remember her smiling.

Marriages in our society need setting up and they need the respective families to agree. This is often more important than the bride agreeing. For my generation in northern Pakistan, it would take a brave girl to stand up to the will of her father and brothers. This was not the case for Toor Pekai and me. Our marriage was arranged by our families but we regard it as a love match, because we very much wanted to be together. Malala makes us laugh on this subject of marriage arrangement. "Yes, Aba," she says. "I will have an arranged marriage, but I will be arranging it myself." I think in spirit, at least, Pekai was like this, too. As a young teenager, if news spread that a man's wife had died and that he was looking for a new bride—much as my own father had—she would rush home quickly to make her feelings known before her family had a chance to even contemplate marrying her off to an old man.

I married Toor Pekai when I was twenty-four. She is still unclear about when she was born because, being a girl, nothing was noted on paper, but we think she is roughly the same age as me. We were engaged for three long years—I was in agony. Her honor meant that I could not hold her photograph next to my heart while I was away at college, studying first for my bachelor's degree and then my master's, so I took instead a photograph of the famous singer and film star Selma Agha, who I thought looked like Toor Pekai. I would pull out the picture to remind me that she was waiting for me in Karshat.

In marriage, we were perfectly in tune. She believed so passionately in all the things I did, even then in the beginning: helping people, serving my community, education for girls.

My wife was strong, funny, wise, and yet social norms had made her illiterate. And to think I'd singled her out as a match based on her looks alone. And then when Malala arrived, I felt in my heart, "These precious females in my life!" The love I felt for them was enough to move mountains. H_2O equals two parts hydrogen, one part oxygen. It is the same formula for a drop of water as it is for an entire ocean. I tell people now that when

I applied the basic principle of gender equality to my one family, it changed my life. It changed my wife's life. It changed my daughter's life. It changed my sons' lives, and I can say with absolute honesty, as my father grew old and approached his death in 2007, it changed his life, too. We Yousafzais together drowned patriarchy in the river Swat and it brought us all such happiness.

A SECOND CHANCE

All my father needed to change his view of girls was an inspiration, a spark to ignite the goodness and purity within him, and that inspiration was Malala. Now I say to Malala, "Jani, you are a lucky girl. You have had this charisma from day one."

When Malala was born on July 12, 1997, ten years before my father died, Toor Pekai and I were living in Mingora, the biggest city in Swat.

Our families knew that Toor Pekai and I had started to live our lives in a different way. Among all the relatives, we were the couple who were the most liberal, progressive, and enlightened. Toor Pekai enjoyed a freedom moving around Mingora alone that we did not see anywhere else in our extended family. I was criticized for that, and so was she. However, in time, my father began to accept the way we lived and Toor Pekai's family did, too. In the beginning, nobody could understand why I encouraged Toor Pekai to walk out and about on her own. She went to and from places like the hospital, the doctor's, the bazaar, and she never had a male chaperone. When my male friends came to our home, I did not expect or want her to cover the majority of her face. This relaxation of purdah was not normal or acceptable behavior for our families. But I remained firm. In time, when Malala began to have more of a public profile in Pakistan, these aspects of our new way of living actually made our family and friends respect us more, but it was a gradual journey. I am proud of the way that we did not give in to the pressure.

My own attempt to be a new kind of man was well under way when Malala was born. Pekai had helped with this. So it was all the more shocking when my father did not celebrate Malala's birth. We had no money at that time, and because she was a girl, he refused to pay for the Woma, the celebration for relatives when a baby is born that requires meat from a goat and rice. I was a struggling teacher and had barely enough money to feed us, so Malala went without her celebration. As far as my father was concerned, it was the curse of our autumn house again— same problem, just different generation, different location. But Malala was to bring about a great change in him.

Even as an infant, Malala had what I call her magnetic field. Neighbors fought to hold her, and when Toor Pekai took her back to Karshat, her village, Malala's great-grandmother and her great-aunts would sit transfixed by Malala sitting in Toor Pekai's lap. "This girl, she seems to be a special girl, Pekai." "What is she doing with her fingers? It looks like she is counting?" Old female relatives fought to hold Malala.

My father was no different. He could not avoid Malala's power, he simply had to yield to it. I like to think that even as an infant, this was Malala's first act as an influential being, that as a girl baby she was too powerful to be ignored by the many people who had been raised to look away from her. I do believe that social norms are like shackles that enslave us. We are content in that slavery, and then when we break the shackles, the first feeling of liberation might be shocking at first, but as we begin to feel the freedom we sense in our souls how rewarding it is.

This is what happened to my father. As a family—three initially, Toor Pekai, Malala, and me—and then four with Khushal, and then towards the end of my father's life, finally five with Atal, we used to visit my father and second mother in Barkana by the brightly colored Flying Coach for the Eid holidays, dressed in our best clothes, laden with bags and gifts. While we were there, Malala and Toor Pekai were confined to the women's quarters while we men and boys were served food and drink by the women, just as I always remembered it. But it was when my father and mother (I called my second mother Khaista Bibi from the start) came to visit us in Mingora that we saw a real change in him. It was a case of my house, my rules. He submitted to our new way of doing things readily. I genuinely believe that he saw how wonderful it was that we were all together, eating together, walking together, enjoying one another. He saw that loving in this manner brought benefits, that it is truly rewarding because it brings joy. I often want to say to men who live in ways that do not value women, "Have you any idea how much greater joy and happiness *you* will have in your hearts if you make this change?"

My father had never eaten with a woman at his table, but we Swat Yousafzais ate our meals together. Toor Pekai was still deeply respectful of him, separating his fish from the bones to spare him the task. "I will pray for you," he told her, so full of gratitude.

When I became politically active in Mingora, sometimes I would not even be there at mealtimes and my father would eat and talk with the women on his own.

As Malala grew older, her personality shone through—bright and vocal and articulate. She began to really excel in her school-work. My father reveled in her academic success. His small granddaughter was so good at everything. She excelled in her Islamic education and her knowledge of the Holy Quran, and he would sing, "Here is Malala / She is like Malalai of Maiwand / But she is the happiest girl in the world."

My father saw the special qualities in Malala, saw how much we respected her and valued her, and because of this he discovered that a girl is just as worthy as a boy.

When Malala came in second in a speech competition at school, he would ask, "Why has not this brilliant girl stood first?" He had aspirations and expectations for Malala in ways that were completely new for him, the father of five girls from whom he had expected nothing. And because he loved Malala and showed her kindness, Malala loved him so much in return, enriching his life with her love.

In the last decade of his life, my father enjoyed this cycle of goodness. When he visited us in Mingora, we would picnic on the banks of the river Swat, which I regard as one of the most beautiful rivers I have ever seen. It crawls from upper Swat to lower Swat and the water is crystal clear, white and blue mixed together. In the distance, the peaks of the Hindu Kush disappear into the clouds, and beside the river, there are lush green fields lined with trees, wildflowers, and rock carvings of ancient gods, the only remains of the second-century Buddhist monasteries that once lined the banks. If I close my eyes, I can take myself back to that riverbank and all its happiness, the air rich with the smell of rice crops planted in the nearby fields.

The riverbank would be full of families like us, released from work for the weekend. It was only two miles or so from our home, but with three generations of us, the walk was not possible. Instead we would take a rickshaw or a small bus, armed with pots of chicken, fish, and rice from home. We seven—my family of five and my mother and father—would cross the river by a lift car to the other side, where the grass was green and lush. Malala and the boys would splash in the river Swat or play ball, and my father would sit on the grass beside us, sometimes using his prayer mat for prayers and other times praying without it. We would stay for hours, and the sun would fall behind the mountains on the horizon and turn the sky crimson. It was so sublime, so romantic, and I used to feel as if I were the luckiest man alive, like we were living in this very special and blessed part of Mother Earth, being loved by one another and by nature, living in the lap of beauty. Before the Taliban came, at first in a gentle way and then more violently in 2007, the year of my father's death, and threatened our beautiful land, I would stand on the riverbank and cry, "Oh, the world is so beautiful!"

There was no difference between any of us on the banks of the river Swat. Moving to Mingora allowed me to grow socially, culturally, and intellectually. When I think of it now, I think of all of us there together. I think of Malala, the first female to open my father's mind to the power of a girl. As he watched Malala grow, I think it dawned on him that supporting a girl brought its own rewards, because it brought him on our new journey. My father saw me dreaming for my daughter, and he joined me in those dreams so that by the end of his life, my father and I dreamed our dreams together.

Sons

THE KITE FIGHTERS

WHEN KHUSHAL AND ATAL were young boys living in Mingora, they would climb onto the roof of our rented house and fly their kites. There would be many boys up there with them, running and shouting and catching the wind, their hands expertly steering the kite lines so that our patch of sky, with the many mountains in the distance, was a beautiful flapping quilt of color.

Kite flying provided a bond between Malala's brothers, as it does between many boys in Pakistan, Afghanistan, and India. Looking back now, from a different land where kite flying is not a national sport, I imagine the freedom my small boys must have felt, standing on the top of the building as the sun began to sink on the horizon and the wind picked up. They were always trying to get the best wind up there on the roof. The strength of the wind and how far it would take their kites was their only concern.

They often worked as a pair. Atal might hold the kite for

Khushal while Khushal moved as far away as he could with the string, and then give his brother the crucial instruction to release the kite into air. And then Khushal would run, reducing the distance between them so that the kite could get picked up by the wind.

What they loved most were kite fights, where they worked as a team against other pairs of boys in the neighborhood, each team trying to cut a rival's kite out of the sky by an expert maneuver involving the tangling and slicing of strings.

Our kites are not like European kites—the strings are not cotton but are coated with crushed glass or metal so that they can cut another line with ease. Pakistan used to be full of organized kite-fighting competitions, which were later banned for safety reasons after stories appeared on the news of treacherous strings falling and injuring those below.

For the boys, it was an innocent sport but intensely competitive. I rarely flew kites in my childhood, so I could not grasp the expertise involved in these kite fights, but Khushal loved them. He would often be on the roof for hours, trying to get his kite higher than his friend's or trying to bring other kites out of the sky completely. The sun would turn his skin a dark chocolate brown, and Toor Pekai would always worry that he was getting dehydrated. But no health worries or grumbles about their neglected bookwork could bring the boys down from the roof.

Sometimes, they would burst through the door, shouting and laughing with a rival kite in their hands. Claiming a rival kite, and then chasing it through the Mingora streets, catching it, and finally bringing it into *your* house as a trophy, was the ultimate triumph.

If Malala's competitiveness was about beating her clever school friends, for the boys it was about kites.

Mingora made the boys as happy as it made me. As a young man beginning to form my own ideas about how I wanted to live my life, the Swat Valley, in all its beauty, had given me so much. But more important than anything, it had helped me become myself. I had discovered first in Spal Bandai and then, after marriage, in Mingora with Toor Pekai, people with whom I could talk politics and write poetry.

When Toor Pekai and I began to have a family, the beauty of our world mirrored the love inside our walls.

I do feel that all families are, in their own way, institutions, undeclared informal institutions. We all have values, however much they differ from family to family. These values are not like charts on the wall, with bullet points. They are both spoken and unspoken and they fill the house. As parents, we hope they are adopted and practiced by every member of the family.

As I became the father of sons as well as a daughter, I defined my family as one that believed first and foremost in equality. We did not write on the walls of our house, "All women and men are equal, all have freedom of speech," but our lives together echoed those values.

Though the boys' births were celebrated by our extended family and the community in the way that Malala's was not, I was determined not to treat them any differently than her.

I was determined to raise a family in which all three children saw no preference between genders.

I also wanted a family that believed in freedom of expression. I had learned from my father not to be demanding of a child who had something to express, whatever it was, from either their mind or their heart.

But how was I to maintain these new values, living deep in a patriarchal society, when all around my boys were other boys and men who were schooled in the old ways?

The way I thought about it was that if my sons saw me behaving a certain way, they would think that way was normal. If they saw that their mother could walk to the bazaar alone, that her voice was as valid as mine, that I respected her and loved her for who she was rather than for the roles and duties she performed for me, that there were no limits on their sister's future, then surely this would set them on a different road themselves.

I believe that all children learn from what we do, not from what we teach. For our children, the role models had to be Toor Pekai and me. If Khushal and Atal could see me treating their mother and their sister with respect and a sense of equality, then that would help groom them to be the kind of men who would practice the same respect for the next generation. That is how I believe social change comes about. It starts with you.

But to have constantly said to the boys with the fervor that I felt in my heart, "You are all human beings. There is no difference, no superiority. We are all equals," when all they really wanted to be doing was flying their kites, could have been counterproductive.

So I never told them that they were supposed to treat Malala equally. I just did it myself. I acted upon the things I believed in. It is such a good starting point.

"Ziauddin," I told myself, "you do not need to give the boys lectures. Just live your normal life. Have love. Have love."

And love is what? Love is freedom. Love is respect. Love is

equality. Love is justice. "So," I told myself, "love your wife and be loved by her, and your children will learn from that." I clung to this when the Taliban invaded our valley and filled our world with hatred and fear.

THE STOLEN CUP

As a family, we had a decade of undisturbed happiness after Malala's birth in 1997, followed by those of Khushal in 2000 and Atal in 2004. This was the period when we would picnic with my father by the river Swat and laugh and tease one another, with Toor Pekai amusing us all with her mimicry of this person or that. She was an excellent mimic even as a small child and, growing up, had been considered one of the most entertaining, lively children in Karshat. Her dry, sharp humor and the blunt way in which she expressed herself were undiminished and, for the children, she was an excellent contrast to me. I continued to enjoy poetry and see the world in ways that were perhaps less practical than the lens through which Toor Pekai did.

I was busy running my school, the Khushal School. It was financially stable by then and full of girls whom, like Malala, I aspired to motivate towards achievement and self-belief. How I loved going from class to class, talking to the children about poetry, listening to them when they told me about the state of their lives and whether their parents were supporting them. I was very active in the community, with various councils and political groups. Life was good.

Khushal and Atal were different from Malala from the start. Malala was a studious child, always running in and out of the classrooms of my school as an infant and working so hard once she became a student herself, surrounded by her books.

Academically, she was a hard act to follow. She was determined to win cups and prizes whenever she could. The education system in Pakistan is all about such things, placing pupil against pupil in the spirit of competition, even small children. It can be very stressful for them, as I remembered from my own childhood.

I never aspired for my children to be the best, although I will admit I enjoyed it. I did not put pressure on them in that way. All I wanted was that they work hard, so I told them, "It doesn't matter if you come first, second, third, whatever. It does not matter, as long as you have tried."

All three of the children were educated in my own school, and this meant I saw firsthand their successes and disappointments. But Malala did not usually have many disappointments. She almost always came first or second. She used to take great care with every examination paper, every book. She made a log of everything. All was neat and tidy and nothing was thrown away. She took after my father in that respect.

But the boys needed more support. Once, in an assembly, I watched tears fill Atal's eyes and roll down his face when the prize he thought was coming to him went to the boy beside him. He was so distraught in the classroom afterwards that his teacher had to come and find me so that I could console him.

Although their grades were not as good as Malala's, I wanted the boys to feel valued for who they were. I did not want them to feel worthless, as I had been made to feel in my schooling, the poor boy with a stammer in a classroom of rich boys favored by the teachers for their birth. But at the same time, I was a head teacher. I loved education. I loved learning. I had gotten my own teachers' attention by getting good marks. Education had saved me.

The boys, to be honest, mostly just wanted to play cricket and go up to the roof to fly their kites. They were not interested in schoolwork.

As a young child, Khushal had some health problems that preoccupied Toor Pekai greatly, and it coincided with a time in which Malala's strengths were becoming more and more apparent. Atal was happy and sociable from birth, and to this day he remains that same funny, happy, smart boy.

Khushal, now eighteen, was a complicated boy, and I say this now when my relationship with him is the most loving and happy it has ever been. But it has not always been that way.

I was always pestering him to read. "Khushal, it is my dream that I come home and I see you reading a book, because you never read any books," I would say irritably if I saw him watching television or playing on his small computer game, or if I returned home and Toor Pekai told me he had been up on the roof flying his kite for hours without taking anything to drink.

One afternoon following the end of school—schools in Pakistan end early, a fact that continues to grieve the boys now that they are in UK schools, which finish much later—Toor Pekai came into the room to find him on the sofa surrounded by books, with a book held in his hand. This was an event! "Khushal!" she exclaimed. "You are reading a book?"

He replied, "No, actually I am not reading. I am fulfilling the dream of my father that I am reading." When Toor Pekai told me this, I burst into laughter. It was good to hear Khushal's clever wit at my expense. There is a message here though: the dreams of your parents can be a burden. I, of all people, who had lived with the looming dread of failing to become a doctor, should have known that.

I spent more time with Khushal and Atal on their schoolwork than I ever had with Malala, but this was because Malala motivated herself. When it came to speeches, learning them, delivering them, I had great success with Atal, who was brilliant in debating competitions and is a born lawyer, but Khushal was not interested in becoming an orator.

Once, I found out that Khushal was about to win a cup for his academic work. I phoned Toor Pekai, who was in Shangla at the time with the children. "He has won!" We were so happy for his sake. It was not the last time that Khushal would prove to me that he was a child who could motivate himself.

On his return to school, Khushal collected his cup, but as he walked home a boy snatched it from his hands and ran off down the crowded street. When Khushal fell through the door of our home, he was crying so hard that Toor Pekai could not make out what had happened. The cup was gone. Toor Pekai flew out of our house and ran through the streets looking for the thief. I have no doubt she would have gotten the cup back if she had found him. She had no luck. Khushal was inconsolable.

When Malala learned of this, she handed Khushal one of her many cups and said she would stick his name on it.

It was a kind act, but of course Khushal wanted the cup he'd won himself.

FATHERS WHO FORGET THEY WERE SONS

The violent Talibanization of the Swat Valley began in 2007, and in late December 2008 the Taliban leader, Maulana Fazlullah, broadcast on Mullah FM, the movement's radio station, that from January 15, 2009, no girl would be allowed to go to school. Teachers started to fall away in fear.

The education of my sons was not affected by this decree. But Malala and all the other girl students in my school would have to stay at home, waiting to be married, waiting for a life of serving their husbands, hidden behind a veil.

How could I bear this as the father of a girl who loved to learn and who had helped build a family in which our very principles of life were freedom and equality? I had filled our family home with crucial values: to be loving, to be kind, to be considerate to other people, to be helpful, to be equal, to be just. And I was now heading back to a way of life as it had been in my own childhood, when my sisters had been forgotten and ignored and I had been celebrated. I had always felt a deep bond with Malala, and the Taliban's ban on her education only reinforced my resolve. Malala was a girl born in a patriarchal society. I *was* more focused on Malala than I was on her brothers because they had been born into a society that favored them. From the time of Malala's birth, I was fighting prejudice against her. By the time Khushal and Atal were born, we could afford the Woma ceremony that Malala had not had. However, I reasoned, "Why should the boys be any different?" So neither of the boys had this important celebration, either. It was the same with the cradle they slept in. If Malala's secondhand cradle was good enough for her, then each of the boys could have it, too. It was as if the imbalance of our society lurked always in the back of my mind, calling out to be corrected.

But recently I have thought, "Why did I prevent my sons from having a ceremony? Their births were worth celebrating every bit as much as Malala's was." The inequalities we saw around us every day were not their fault. Why must they not be celebrated? Boys have needs, too.

Perhaps I can allow myself to feel this now because Malala is so successful. I feel that empowering girls must not come at the expense of disempowering boys. Enlightened, confident young boys, loved by their families, taught to value themselves and respect their sisters, their mothers, and their female classmates, grow up to be good men and help bring about change. How Khushal and Atal viewed girls and women while they were children would shape their view of women and girls in their adulthood.

But the Talibanization of our homeland meant that I was preoccupied with protecting our rights, not analyzing or thinking proactively. It was all about defending what little we already had for the girls.

The Taliban was such a powerful enemy, and its pronouncements about women and girls' education were so hateful and devastating for the lives of women and girls, that my need to speak out against them strengthened my bond with Malala. It became our mission.

We were slowly to become co-campaigners in a way that did not involve the boys. We were all united in this campaign, particularly Toor Pekai, who gave us her blessing and, crucially, supported us with her wisdom and calm, but she was not visible because, culturally, she could not be. Our patriarchal culture together with the effects of Talibanization made women prisoners inside the four walls of their homes.

The boys were not old enough to really understand what was happening to Mingora. What they did understand, they acted out on the rooftop of our house, playing soldiers with guns trying to shoot each other, the Taliban against the army. To them, it was as harmless a game as the kite flying.

In the years between 2007 and October 9, 2012, when Malala was attacked, I was so busy campaigning, delivering speeches, and attending councils and meetings, either alone or with Malala, that sometimes I did not focus much on the boys. When the Taliban was not burning our schools or flogging people in the squares or murdering my friends, its members were always in our lives, wandering around, a reminder of what might or could happen to any one of us.

My sons' education was extremely important to me, but it was not as remarkable for its very existence as Malala's was. Boys had been acquiring an education in Pakistan for decades. And so it was Malala and I who went on this kind of girl-journey, this girl-odyssey, together. Our campaign to save girls' education in our country lasted for five years, until she was shot, by which point she was the most influential teenager in Pakistan.

It was during this period that Khushal took aside one of my close friends, Ahmad Shah, and told him, "My father is not taking care of me like he is taking care of Malala." It pained me so much when my friend repeated this to me. It was such a big shock because my relationship with Khushal was good. I had taken an interest in his studies and helped him with his reading.

Every day as a parent you try to be good. It is a kind of investment in the future, because parenthood does go on and on, its effects shaping future generations of your family. It is why family life is so important.

As a parent, day to day, you can get it wrong when you think you are getting it right. It is moments like Khushal's complaint to my friend that remind me that parenthood is difficult. I had thought, "I am a fine father for them all." I could see that as Malala became more famous in our country for her campaign, Khushal might have thought, "Maybe it is my father who is making her famous." But I told him that really it was Malala who invited that interest in me, and not only in me but in many people in our community. She had a special gift for campaigning and delivering speeches. Malala is unique in her talents—I am not—but then she was a child who needed an adult companion. That made us unique.

Khushal's words stung me, and I tried my hardest to redress the imbalance, but I had not the time, in truth, because I was so taken up with my own stand against the Taliban. In this, I failed Khushal in a way that my father never failed me. My father might not have had money, but he gave me his full attention. He made time. I was so preoccupied with what was happening to my country that when we temporarily became internally displaced persons in 2009, when the Pakistani army came to Mingora to clear out the Taliban, I even forgot Malala's twelfth birthday. We all did.

In 2011, the year before Malala was attacked, the same year she won Pakistan's National Youth Peace Prize and Osama bin Laden was killed in Abbottabad, Toor Pekai and I made a bad decision about Khushal's future. At the beginning of 2012, a terrible year because of Taliban death threats, we sent him miles away to attend and board at a very good school, also in

Abbottabad. As is so often the case, we thought we were making this decision for his own good. We wanted the best for Khushal and Atal in the same way that we wanted the best for Malala. At least our boys could benefit from a good education in the many schools for boys. In Pakistan, the best schools for boys are often considered to be the cadet schools run by the army. Girls were not able to attend these schools when Malala was growing up, although since 2014, a cadet school for girls has opened in Marden, a sign that change in our country is happening slowly. We decided that in order to prepare Khushal for entry into a cadet school, he must attend a private preparatory school. We chose Abbottabad, hours away from the Swat Valley, because it was more peaceful. From the beginning, Khushal did not want to go, but I compelled him.

I believed it was my duty to give Khushal what I felt he needed. I was looking out for him. It was an expensive decision—the fees were much more than I had ever spent on Malala's education—and it was an expensive mistake.

Malala was doing so well at the Khushal School. She was such a good student, but I felt my son Khushal needed this extra push from a better school. Why did I not listen to Khushal? He hated it from the start. He cried all the time. The teachers hit the boys—not an uncommon thing in schools in Pakistan at that time. It was traumatic for him.

Every phone call he begged us to collect him, saying that he would run away. "You have put me in a jail," he shouted down the line. Toor Pekai was often distraught. We all missed him, Toor Pekai especially. I missed him desperately, too, but I clung to this bigger picture I had for him: good school, good college, good job, secure future.

He must have stayed there for two or three months and then finally during a second visit home he refused to go back. It was a display of the character strength we'd hoped to give all the children.

"This time I will not do it," Khushal said. "I'm here." He meant it.

I had to yield, even though it had been an expensive initiative. But I did not want him to think of me as a bad father, or feel I had treated him in a bad way. I wanted to be remembered as a responsible, kind, good father.

It has made me think that when parents' dreams for their children are against their children's wishes, when they threaten to take over the happiness of the present, these dreams can infringe on the basic rights of every child. We parents think we know best, that we can decide for the best, but we are not always right.

Khushal had been so used to the love of us all, to his friends, to his life in Mingora. How could I have thought of uprooting him for the sake of a bright future for him of my own making? My father had done that to me! I should have known better.

Every father has been a son in his time, but fathers can forget they have been sons. There is a line from Khalil Gibran that I feel sums up what I was only to learn in the fullest and truest extent later. And I learned it the hard way. "Your children are not your children / They are the sons and daughters of Life's longing for itself / They come through you but not from you, /And though they are with you yet they belong not to you."

Almost immediately on Khushal's return, Khushal and Atal were back up on the roof together, the kites dancing in the wind.

Khushal was never going to leave again, he told us. We never wanted to leave our beautiful Swat Valley, either.

The morning of October 9, 2012, over our usual breakfast of chapatis, fried egg, and the sugary sweet tea I love, Toor Pekai had ordered Atal to travel home on the school bus with Malala. She was extremely nervous about the safety of all the children, and she would never really relax until they were back home with her. The bus was driven by Usman Bhai Jan, a funny man who would amuse the children with magic tricks and comic stories. Atal, too, was a funny and a cheeky boy, an equal match for Usman. He could also be very badly behaved on this bus ride from the Khushal School to our home. He often refused to sit on the seats inside the bus with the girls, wanting instead to hang dangerously off the back as the bus wound its way through the potholed streets of Mingora. He was only eight and light as a feather. Usman worried, not without reason, that one false move down a deep pothole and Atal's body would be flung off the back of the bus, causing him great injury or even death.

That lunchtime, on Pekai's orders, Atal walked over from the primary school in order to meet up with Malala. I had been in the school that morning, not in Malala's part, where she was doing some exams, but in Atal's primary division. By lunchtime, I had left to attend a rally meeting at the Swat Press Club in my capacity as president of the Private Schools Association. Pekai was at home, preparing to leave for an English lesson.

Usman arrived outside the school with his *dyna,* or open-backed van, as normal. Malala stood with her friends in their school uniforms, and among the large group of teenage girls in their shalwar kamizes and their school scarves, there was little

Atal, weaving in and out, full of mischief and energy. As the girls climbed into the back of the dyna, Atal refused to be seated. "Atal Khan, if you do not sit inside, I will not take you at all," Usman Bhai Jan told him. Usman remembers this being the one day when he'd had enough of the stress of driving Atal home in such an unsafe manner. But Atal would rather walk home than admit defeat, and after a short standoff in which Atal attempted to argue himself into being allowed to ride on the tailboard, Usman made the decision to drive off without him. As Atal stood and watched the dyna disappear down the Haji Baba Road, its wheels kicking up dirt and dust, he was furious. Atal does not like to lose a fight. I do not like the idea at all that Atal made Usman Bhai Jan's job of driving the school bus more difficult than it already was. By 2012, it had been three years since the Pakistani army had cleared the Taliban from Mingora, but there were still army soldiers and checkpoints, which the dyna had to pass at least four times a day. But given what was about to happen, I look back now and I think, "Thank God Atal's naughtiness banned him from the bus that day." Atal himself says, "Aba, I was lucky I was not on that bus."

As Atal began walking home with his friends, Usman drove the dyna along its usual route, up the Haji Baba Road, turning right at the army checkpoint and then continuing along a hilly road, a busy shortcut that Usman thought seemed oddly deserted. On any other day, hanging off the back of the dyna, Atal would have been the first to see the two young men step forward from the side of the road to stop the bus. While the first boy remained at the front trying to distract Usman, the second moved to the back, where Atal would have been. "Who is Malala?" the boy asked everybody sitting inside. When all eyes went involuntarily to my daughter, this boy raised his gun and pulled the trigger. The bullet hit Malala in the head and then hit her two friends, Shazia and Kainat.

Malala remembers nothing of this attack. All Atal remembers of Pakistan is the happiness of flying his kite, but had Usman allowed him to travel on the tailboard that day, Atal might have been damaged forever by seeing his sister shot at point-blank range. Who is Malala? As the body of my courageous daughter fell forward and her blood hit the seats and floor of the dyna, Atal would have thought, "Malala is my sister and now she is dead."

There was to be no more kite flying for the boys ever again. Usman drove the dyna at top speed to Swat Central Hospital. I had turned off my phone to give a speech, but my friend at the Swat Press Club received the call that the Khushal School bus had been hit. I was in a state of confusion. Could Malala have been hurt? Was Atal on the bus that day?

I went onstage and made my excuses. Another friend took a call. Malala had been hurt. I have told the story of that day many times in the past six years, but it never gets any easier. *Oh my God. Oh my God.* I rushed in my friend's car to find Malala at the hospital lying on a bed. "Oh, my brave daughter, my brave Malala, my brave, brave girl." I said these words as I kissed her forehead, which had been wrapped in a bandage and was now wet with blood. I could not cry. I could not shed one tear. I think I was beyond crying. The only way I can describe it was like being sucked into a deep black hole. I was out of the frame of space and time. I was like a stone, utterly blank. A helicopter was summoned to take her to a much bigger hospital in Peshawar. I ran beside the stretcher as it was taken to the helipad in Mingora less than a mile from our home. It feels odd to watch the television footage of this now. As we flew over the landscape, I was indifferent to it. Malala was beside me vomiting blood. "Please God, please God, let her survive." I begged. At home, on her prayer mat, Pekai, after hearing the news, began reciting from the Quran. "Do not cry," she told the many women who had flocked to our house. "Pray." When Atal came through the door, he switched on the television and saw the footage. He began weeping and called for Khushal. Together they watched the news ticker running along the bottom of the television broadcasts, preparing for the words "Pakistani teenager Malala Yousafzai declared dead." We had all watched this happen with Benazir Bhutto in 2007.

Three days later, after lifesaving surgery at Combined Military Hospital Peshawar, and then more care in the Armed Forces Institute of Cardiology in Rawalpindi, at 5 a.m. on Monday, October 15, Malala was taken in an ambulance under armed escort to Rawalpindi airport, to a waiting private UEA plane. The roads were closed and snipers lined the streets. Her stretcher was wheeled on board and she was soon in the skies again, being flown far away to a hospital, the Queen Elizabeth, in an unknown city called Birmingham, in the United Kingdom. This hospital was to provide her with the vital care that, if we were very lucky, might limit the damage the bullet had inflicted on her brain.

As we waited to leave Pakistan to follow her, Khushal burst into tears at the table and shouted, "We were five and now we are four!" It had not been written anywhere on our walls that our family would always be five, just as we had had no need to write down, "We are all equal," but it was a truth. We had always been five. And then we were not.

The boys' kites are still there in Mingora, in a box, their

strings intact, along with Malala's bed and her school trophies, certificates, awards, books, and reports, proof of the education she fought to keep.

Our family home is now rented by another family. One room has been allocated for our possessions, packed up for us in our absence, relics of the happy life we had there.

THE BEAUTIFUL CHANGES

When I was a boy, playing cricket on the muddy roof of our shack, my father would call my name, "Ziaaaaaaaaaaa—udina!" And before he had even finished the last syllable, I was down by his side. I would just be there before him, so obedient, like an army soldier to the call of his officer shouting, "Attention!" But as my sons became teenagers in the West, I did not see that automatic obedience in either of them and I will admit that I wanted it. I needed it.

I would call up the stairs that dinner was ready only for my calls to be met with silence. Had they not heard me? Often I would climb the stairs of our house in Birmingham, which felt so strange with its marble surfaces and empty rooms, and open the doors to their bedrooms to find both boys hunched over their computer screens, in a cloud of blue light. "Did you not hear me?" I would ask. Sometimes they would not even look at me. And I would tell this story of my childhood again and again: "When I was a boy, playing cricket..." It made no difference. "Why are you not like the son I was to my father?" I would say to Khushal, who I felt was old enough to understand that I deserved respect.

It was always computers, Xboxes, Game Boys, phone apps. I did not understand these gadgets, let alone know how to use them. My first experience on a computer was when I was thirty-five.

"Why are you ignoring me?" I would say angrily to the boys. I was so frustrated. Khushal seemed to be growing up fast.

Where had the liberal Ziauddin gone? The father who saw the error of his ways back in Pakistan and believed in equality and freedom and in encouraging his sons to express themselves? Where had the Ziauddin gone who craved a new, softer, freer upbringing for his boys? For about two and a half years, that Ziauddin could not be found anywhere. I could not find him.

Separated from our culture, from our family, from a support structure full of my friends and Toor Pekai's friends, people who might well have been mentors to our children, I really struggled with the boys. They were living a Western life in the UK that I did not recognize. I, a Muslim father from South Asia, had a fear in my heart that I was going to lose my sons. This is not uncommon among Asian parents and I understand it.

I saw that the gap between us was becoming so much bigger than the gap between my father and me had ever been. For all my modernizing as a young man, I had remained obedient and respectful. Although I had learned English and understood the importance of equality, the bridge between my father and me was our faith, our love of the great Urdu and Pashto writers, and ultimately that I had never challenged his authority. My mission had been about giving Malala power, not taking power away from my father with disrespect.

Did I revert to an authoritarian type of fathering in fear? Or was it that the boys, now exposed to a society with different values, were less inclined towards obedience and my final word? "You crazy boys," I'd say to them. "You don't listen to me." And I was not joking. But the boys were not living the life I had led at their age, nor even the life they would have led had we stayed in Pakistan. They were forging, or trying to forge, their own paths in a new world.

There was a different problem at the beginning. When we arrived in Britain, the boys were traumatized, particularly Khushal. Dr. Fiona Reynolds, the Birmingham intensive care pediatrician who by coincidence had happened to be in Pakistan when Malala was attacked and who had helped save her life, remembers the first time she saw the boys. They were in bunk beds in Rawalpindi, while we waited to be flown to the UK. Atal was fast asleep, but Khushal, she told me later, was the most terrified child she had ever seen.

The boys did not go to school in the UK until well into the year following our arrival. They spent most of their time on computer games, first in the hospital hostel and then in the apartment on the tenth floor of a block in the middle of Birmingham. There was nothing for them to do. They were bored. Toor Pekai and I talked only of Malala's treatment, her recovery. For us, there *was* nothing else to talk about.

Khushal was thirteen and would shout at the computer screen. He broke eight controllers. I cannot remember how we came to have eight controllers. Atal played computer games, too, and ate sweets. Neither of them understood anything about their lives. They were frightened boys.

"I was just following everyone else. I didn't know what I was doing. Everything was hardening" is how Atal explained it to me later. On one occasion at the hospital, at a time when Malala was suffering dreadful headaches and brain fluid was leaking out of her ears, he shouted, "Give me my passport. I demand my passport. I am going home to Pakistan."

We were all crying.

As if helping to save Malala's life was not enough of a blessing, Dr. Fiona, along with her husband, Adrian, began taking the boys for outings to integrate them slowly into the Western way of life. They went to the cinema in Birmingham's Bullring, which the boys could hardly believe, and to Warwick Castle, that time with Malala, too. The bullet had made Malala deaf in one ear and cut a facial nerve that caused one side of her face to droop. However, miraculously, it had not affected her memory or her brain or any of her limbs. As Malala started to recover, she joined the boys in these outings. They went bowling, for example, and to Nando's, where they all ate fried chicken.

I should have seen that everything had changed, and that the boys needed to respond to that change in their own way, Instead, after about a year in the UK, my relationship with Khushal started to deteriorate. He had not settled in at school as well as Malala and Atal, and he was still without a close friend, which the other two had found. He missed his life in Pakistan so much, his old friends, his kite, his life the way it used to be. To be honest, I missed Pakistan, too. Toor Pekai missed Pakistan. Malala missed Pakistan. The only person who did not was Atal, who quickly lost the memories that flooded the rest of us.

Khushal was also old enough to understand what had happened to his sister. He is a deep thinker and an emotional boy, and he recognized the Taliban's hatred. Atal, our sharp bright arrow, was too young. Luck had spared him from being on the bus that fateful day. Surrounded by his new friends, he picked up English with no problems at all. Soon, it was as if he had been born in Britain.

Schoolwork seemed a low priority. Khushal was always playing those addictive games. I'd hear him through the door talking to somebody, but nobody was in there with him, and then shouting, and I thought, "What is he doing? What will become of this boy?" I found it so unacceptable, and I was scared I was losing him. I wanted him to be a boy who was focused on his studies and learning and giving at least some time to his books. I kept thinking, "When is he going to get fed up with this computer stuff?" It brought out the worst in me.

Teenage boys need a mentor with whom they can explore who they are without fear of judgment or expectation.

In Pakistan, it had been easy for me to be a father to the boys. They were younger then, and they were exposed to a bigger community of people who shared their culture. They used to go to the mosque. They went to their friends' houses and met their cousins in Shangla. We had people around us, talking, cooking, praying, debating ideas.

The change to our family in leaving Pakistan was revolutionary, a 180-degree turn. We had gone from living with a household full of our friends and family to being largely on our own. As Atal told me, we were no longer in a culture where boys immediately ran to get their father a glass of water. The boys were surrounded by children who had different relationships with their parents. There was not this automatic obedience, this emphasis on authority. Away from Pakistan, I saw that I was a Pashtun father. Where I had run from the roof at the very sound of my father shouting "Ziaaaaaaa-udina!" my sons did not come when I called.

I was so sad about this. I blamed myself.

When I was at the exact age Khushal was during this difficult period—around thirteen or fourteen years old—I had a few mentors who guided me away from hatred, away from a dangerous path. One of them had been Toor Pekai's elder brother, and through gentle conversation he brought me back to safety when my beliefs were going astray.

The cleric who was providing me with Islamic instruction believed in jihad and I was being radicalized very successfully. For a very brief period, I wanted a war with the infidels and I wanted to die fighting. I wanted to be a martyr, because this was what I was being taught with the same passion and conviction that I have taught in my life, only in the direction of love.

I look back now and think of Toor Pekai's brother and other progressive friends in my life and my own kind father, and I say to myself, "Ziauddin, without this guidance you could have become a suicide bomber with a belt strapped to your chest!"

I needed a way of being with Khushal, and at the moment I lost faith, Dr. Fiona stepped in again. She was our mentor.

"I am really in trouble," I told her. "Khushal likes you. You like my sons. Please tell me what I can do."

There is no shame in parents asking for help. We talked together and she said, "These changes come in adolescents and you should be ready to cope with this situation in a noble or wise way. Do not lose your temper and try not to be hard on him.

"He is a good boy," she said. "It's a difficult time. He'll be okay. He's bright, he's clever, he's handsome. It will be all right. He is a wonderful boy."

"You are right," I told her. "You are right."

And after that I just gave in. I gave in. I stopped talking about schoolwork, and I stopped expecting obedience. I trusted Dr. Fiona, but I also began to question myself. I wanted to be a good father, a kind father. My way was not working. It was very unfair that I should want the boys to live a life like mine. I felt clear that I wanted to maintain the importance of our family values, those of equality and truth and justice, but anything that I wanted for them beyond this I recognized as being about me and what I wanted for them. Why should I decide if they went to university or read a certain book? Or pursued a certain career path? They were living in a different age and in a different culture.

I had been looking for the kind of obedient son I had been to my father, and Dr. Fiona helped me see that I was searching for the wrong thing. My son was wonderful for who he was, not for how much like me I could make him.

I believe that parenting never stops, and because of that, it requires change or certainly an openness to adaptation. Dr. Fiona talked to Khushal for hours, calmly waiting for him to calm down if he was angry. She listened to him, but she also pointed out the obvious. There are not many students who do well in school without putting in any effort. If Khushal wanted to get good grades in his GCSEs, he was going to have to start working. Because I had stopped caring about the computer games, very quickly Khushal got bored of them and stopped playing them. These days, it is my own phone that is always ringing and pinging with messages. When once I asked Khushal what he would change about me, he said, "Aba, why this dependence on the phone? Stop looking at it when we have guests! It is so rude!" I said to him, "Khushal Khan, you are right. I am sorry. I cannot help it." He took it out of my hand and threw it down the back of the sofa. It is a funny reversal, I think, given how anxious I was in the past about *their* devices. Now, aged eighteen, it is Khushal who is confiscating my phone rather than the other way around.

With time I also began to understand more about the UK education system. My sons were becoming critical thinkers. And they were not always on the computer just to play. Often, they were doing their homework. I had not understood this.

I stopped worrying and I just loved them. It was such a relief.

As I let go of my expectations of them and my old view of what a son should be, they became my friends. My best friends. I learned that they will find their happiness in a kind of life that is different from what I have known but still informed by all the values of love and kindness and equality that we had in Mingora. Understanding that made my life easy. And it set us free.

YOU SAY BURRITO, I SAY BURRITA

It is rare that I enjoy anything other than Pakistani food, but during one of my recent trips to America, the former communications director of the Malala Fund, Eson Jordan, bought me the most delicious food, a flour tortilla with a filling, which I thought he said was called a burrita. I ate it for breakfast in the back of the taxi as we traveled back to the airport.

The next time I was in America, we were all together in Los Angeles, and I was out in a market with the boys. I spotted a Starbucks coffee shop, and, feeling hungry, I announced, "I'm going in there to buy a burrita."

"Aba," they pleaded, "please do not do this. It is a big mistake. Do not ask for this here."

But I ignored them. "Please, let me check. Maybe they do have one." I was very persistent.

In I went and I said to the manager, "Do you have a b-b-b-b-b-b-b-b—" I became very stuck, very badly stuck, on this word, as I often do with hard sounds. The woman at the counter was so patient. She did not laugh at all. Finally, I managed to get it: a b-b-b-b-b-b-b—burrita! I was triumphant.

The boys were laughing so hard behind me they could hardly stand up straight. The poor manager kept her composure, but she had to tell me kindly that, no, sir, there was no such food sold in Starbucks.

As we left the shop, Atal said to me, "Aba, you made three mistakes." And I said, "How?"

He said, "Number one, you are asking for Mexican food in Starbucks. This you will never find. Number two, it is not burrit-a, it is burrit-o. And number three, your stammer meant that you could not even say this word! You ruined the word twice."

They were laughing so much, and when we rejoined Malala and Toor Pekai, they joined in. Soon after, they set up a Snapchat group among them with the title "burrit-a," and I joined as an honorary member. I enjoyed this teasing, and I shared the story with many of our friends. I enjoyed my children laughing at me. We had discovered how to love one another, and because of this, I was laughing, too.

I think when you laugh at yourself, you become more human and you tell your children that it is okay in life to have weak moments and to accept them as normal. I think it is important to have a sense of humor. If I had been the old Ziauddin, claiming authority and demanding respect, I would have been offended by the burrita teasing and gone off into another room and thought, "I am a father and you are children. Show me some respect!" They would have laughed at me behind my back. Now I do not see the teasing as showing a lack of respect for me. Instead I see it as an embarrassing moment for me that provided a funny story we all enjoyed.

THE CLASS OF MALALA

School exams can be a stressful time for a parent, never mind the student!

In the run-up to Khushal's GCSEs two years ago, I said nothing about the importance of studying. I had learned my lesson and trained myself not to measure him by how much work he appeared to be doing.

Three months before Khushal's exams, he became very serious. He spread his books over the sitting room sofas. Here was chemistry on one, biology on another, computer science and religious studies. When guests came, there was nowhere to sit. He used to say to the guests, "Let's go to the sitting room because this sofa is going to get an A and this sofa is going to get an A." And we all used to laugh.

And then his results came in. It was amazing, really amazing. I was so happy for him.

I was full of regret, too, at my own behavior. My son got fantastic grades and he'd had this potential all along. Dr. Fiona was right.

These days, I am a hugging father for Khushal. Every day he comes and he kisses me on one side of the cheek and then the other. He is the only person in the family who does. Malala and Toor Pekai do not like hugging much. And the kiss from Khushal is a genuine one. It is like the kiss that my father used to give me. It is the same because it is full of love, even though the relationship the boys and I have is entirely different.

We talk about how we used to be, which seems a world away. Khushal has said to me, "You kept on giving me chances. Even if I made a mistake, you gave me a second chance, a third chance, a fourth chance. And I think I began to realize myself that you might have had a point." I have asked him what he thinks a father should be, and he has told me, "A father should build his son's character rather than build his son's mind for him." I think these are wise words and I am glad I understand what they mean now.

I don't see myself as authoritarian, but I hope that I am a figure of respect.

When Atal was about to go out recently, I said, "Atal Khan, should I not know the names of the friends you will be with?" And he responded cheekily, "Aba, I don't ask you for a list of *your* friends' names, do I?" I laughed so hard. How could I argue?

There is not a tradition of the "sleepover" in Pakistan. When Atal first asked us to invite his friends to stay, Toor Pekai and I were confused. I said to him "What does that mean, sleepover? Why would these boys sleep in our home when they have beds of their own?" But Atal explained to us, "Look, my friends will come over and they will sleep at our house." And I said, "Why?" And he said, "Because it is a tradition here."

And we said, "Oh, okay." And they came, about eight boys of

different colors and religions, and they were up all night, maybe until 3 a.m., and they were just talking and playing in Atal's room, but I was so happy.

If these friends make Atal happy, then there are one hundred extra blessings of love filling my house.

Loving my sons unconditionally has meant that they came to respect me naturally. I learned that real authority is not found in fear but in this respect. We no longer call Dr. Fiona "Aunty" but say "Godmother" instead, a tribute to the guidance she continues to give the boys. It is Malala who is Khushal's newest mentor. Where once they fought over the television remote control, now they talk about his life, his plans to follow her to Oxford—"If you come, I'll leave!" she tells him in jest—and affairs of Khushal's heart. They text each other every day. Aged fourteen, Atal, that small disobedient boy, is almost as tall as Malala. "My sister is brilliant," he says. "I should not be scared to be in her shadow. I should learn from her and how she does this special thing. I should learn not to be afraid like she is not afraid. Not to be shy and how to get my words across. People might say I am in her shadow, but I think rather that I am in her class. I am in the class of Malala, and I am learning from her."

My grandfather and my father would never have thought that it would be a girl in the family who would be mentoring her brothers in this way.

I thank God for these beautiful changes.

Wife and Best Friend

An event at Khushal School and College, 2010.

Receiving awards at the annual prize ceremony from then education secretary Mehmood Hahn, Jehanzeb College, Swat.

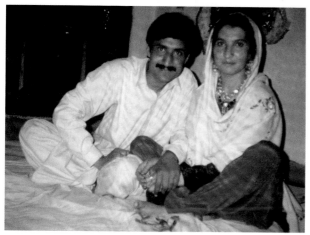

My wife, Toor Pekai, and me as newlyweds in Shangla.

Toor Pekai and me holding Malala and Khushal on the bank of the river Swat, around 2001.

My father, Rohul Amin, laughing with his three grandchildren, Malala, Atal, and Khushal.

Holding Atal, with Malala.

Talking at morning school assembly in Mingora in 2008.

Dr. Fiona, mentor to my two sons, enjoying fish and chips in the gardens of Warwick Castle, June 2013.
Copyright Adrian Bullock

Our family and Kailash Satyarthi's in Oslo after the presentation of the Nobel Peace Prize 2014 to Kailash and Malala.

Eating corn on the cob with Malala in Santa Barbara, California.

Speaking to an all-girl secondary school in Maasai Mara, Kenya, sponsored by Free the Children.

Building a wall at a school in Maasai Mara, Kenya, with Malala and Craig Kielburger, cofounder of Free the Children.

Meeting Syrian refugees in Jordan.

With Malala at the Maasai Mara safari park in Kenya.

Islamabad, 2018: Malala receiving a kiss from my mother, Maharo Bibi, with her maternal grandmother, Del Pasanda, next to her, as Toor Pekai, Toor Pekai's brothers, and I watch from behind.

Malala meeting her uncle, my brother Saeed Ramzan, in Islamabad.

My nephew Mubashir Hassan with Khushal, Malala, and Atal.

At our old family house in Mingora, sitting in front of Malala's school trophy cabinet.

2018: An emotional moment after landing at the same helipad in Swat from which a wounded Malala was airlifted to Peshawar in 2012.

THE QUIET ACTIVIST

SOMETIMES I ASK MYSELF what would have happened in my life had Toor Pekai not been my wife. I think I would have struggled to bring up children who believed deeply in gender equality like ours do, because how could I have instilled those ideas and values in them if their mother was not part of our family's journey? How would equality have come to mean anything to Malala, Khushal, and Atal if they had seen their mother live in my shadow? There would have been no bridge between us, husband and wife, and no bridge between Pekai and her children. In countries where there is a strong patriarchy, change has to come from women, too. So many women all over the world are told from birth that men are more important. There comes a time when they have to actively stop believing this and claim what they are entitled to. This is why I call Toor Pekai my co-traveler.

Toor Pekai was—is—so important in the role of mother

because she refused to chain Malala with all the lessons she herself had been taught about being a girl. In Toor Pekai's childhood, girls were judged only by the honor they brought to the male members of the family—their father, their brothers, and their sons—and their determination never to bring upon the family any kind of shame. "Shame" is not only acting in a bad way. It can be acting in an independent way. If a girl falls in love with a boy not chosen by her parents and meets him unchaperoned, this is considered shameful. Looking into the eyes of a man who is not your husband is a "shame." There is a Pashtun saying that the most honorable girl in the village—in other words the "best" girl—will always keep her eyes to the floor, even when her village is on fire. As a teenager, Pekai asked her mother, "What kind of girl would not look up to help when all around her people and homes are burning?" When faced with this logic, her mother replied, "Oh, Pekai, what can I say?"

It was Pekai, as a woman, who was also courageous in the way she unlearned old ideas about the difference between boys and girls.

Early in our marriage, first in Barkana and then shortly afterwards in Mingora, where we really began our own joint journey towards freedom, I was struggling in life to become a teacher and then to set up my own school. Pekai was so supportive. Even on our honeymoon, which we spent at my father's house, she did not complain when I went off every day to volunteer as a teacher in the high school where once I was a student. Looking back now, I see this is characteristic of her. She is a rock, steady and self-assured, with a heart dedicated to the needs of others.

We never seemed to have any money, and it saddened me so much when Pekai had to sell her wedding bangles. Where could

I find a job, a good opportunity, so that I could earn a living and provide for a future family, while still enjoying a sense of pride from contributing to my community? It seemed hopeless. Neither Pekai nor I wanted to stay in Karshat or Barkana.

Pekai called me "Khaista" from the beginning of our marriage. It means "beautiful one." My nephews called me this, too. I am not beautiful, but it is a lovely pet name that I still like hearing Pekai use. "Khaista," she would say, "if you do these good things for others, God will ensure that we are okay."

After a period of teaching English in a well-known private college in Mingora, I set up my own school with an old college friend called Muhammad Naeem. He was later replaced by another friend, Hidayatullah. It was a mixed primary school, a dream come true for a lower-class man like me who believed so much in education. We had just three pupils. There was nowhere in the school for Pekai and me to live as a married couple, but she joined us and we lived in two dirty rooms I rented near the school. It was in this shack that she gave birth to our first child, a girl. The child was stillborn. Pekai still remembers her, with her pale skin and refined nose. I have always blamed our rooms' lack of hygiene. But Toor Pekai did not complain too much about our conditions. The school was her dream, too. She held the lantern while I whitewashed the school's walls late into the night.

We named the school the Khushal School, after the poet Khushal Khan Khattak, and we painted a motto by the door: "We are committed to build you for the call of the new era." But the new era for us, in reality, meant poverty. I was in a lot of debt from college, and our three students were hardly enough for us to survive.

But being married to Pekai brought me such happiness. As a child, Toor Pekai, had valued her independence. She was a strong character who had loved running around Karshat, the neighboring village to mine, but adolescence and purdah had meant that her movements became restricted and her face was veiled. Marriage and a home in Mingora, however humble, meant she could experience once again the freedoms she had enjoyed as a child. In Mingora, life was different from that in Barkana in that the women seemed more relaxed in their movement from place to place. I was adamant that Pekai enjoy the kind of freedom that would have been impossible for a woman living in either of our villages. She walked around without me, and inside our home we behaved as equals. If a man ever criticized us to my face, I took no notice.

What I discovered was that in feeling Pekai's freedom with me, I, too, felt free. She enriched my life by being herself. Pekai was not a wife who brought the patriarchal burden of needing to be "protected," that is, monitored. The kind of patriarchy we lived with—the kind that does not allow women to have economic independence—forces women to become a burden on their husbands, and then as widows on their brothers. It forces them to live in fear, too, constantly thinking about their honor. But I trusted Toor Pekai, and I was mostly free of the old patriarchal ideas.

There were still the taught old rules of my childhood, however, and sometimes I caught myself behaving like an old-fashioned Pashtun. It was again a case of the old Ziauddin in battle with the new Ziauddin. So I had to defeat the old Ziauddin and accept the new Ziauddin, but it took time to accept my new self. I did not always get it right.

Whenever the old Ziauddin popped up in our marriage, it was Toor Pekai who pushed him down. For example, during the first month after the wedding, while we were still in Shangla, I told her my male friend was coming to visit. As a traditional Pashtun, you are not supposed to allow your friends to meet your wife. It rarely happened. I was happy that Toor Pekai would meet my friend. Pekai knew him because he was in the community, but she had not met him as my wife. When I told her of his visit, she said she would like to make herself presentable with makeup. Instinctively I said, "Why should you be making yourself up for him?" It was the Pashtun in me.

But she challenged me. She said, "It is my right to use makeup. This is my house, too. If you are not comfortable with this, then why bring your friend here?" I felt ashamed. "I am sorry," I told her. "You are right."

On another occasion, a bit later in our marriage, somebody followed us home to where we lived in Mingora. We had visited the home of a new teacher, traveling there and back by rickshaw. Even with my new ideas of equality, I felt self-conscious walking beside Pekai in the street. Women did not walk the streets with their husbands. They went with their brothers and fathers. I quickened my pace, so that Pekai fell behind me, even though we had the same destination. A man followed us and then reported me to the person from whom I rented the school building. There was a knock at our door. When I answered it, the man said to me, "There has been a report that you have brought a woman back here. Can you explain this to me, please?" I said, "That woman is my wife! I rent this building! Do not meddle in my business." I was furious, but in my discomfort at being seen in public with my wife—an endorsement of her freedom—I had acted in a guilty-looking way. Pekai was angry with the man who had followed us, suspecting some abuse of her honor, or that she was some sort of shameful woman. But it was I who had let her down. I should have walked the streets of Mingora with Pekai by my side with pride.

There was one aspect of Pekai's life in which she remained traditional. This was her view of the scarf, which she wore in public in a way that obscured almost all of her face. Until we left Pakistan in 2012 following Malala's attack, she could never bring herself to relax the way she covered her face. I would say to her, "Pekai, purdah is not only in the veil. It is in the heart." When Malala and I began appearing in the media in our campaign against the Taliban, Pekai would never allow herself to be filmed or photographed. The first time she agreed to have her picture taken was in 2013, when Malala gave her speech to the UN in New York on her sixteenth birthday.

Pekai's view of the scarf was connected to her religious devotion and also to the opinions of everybody living around us. Her whole life she had been taught to believe that being a good Muslim means covering yourself from the eyes of men who are not your husband.

Misinterpretations of the Holy Quran that suppress women are how the Taliban attracted female followers at first, because they played on women's desire to always want to be better Muslims.

When the Taliban leader Maulana Fazlullah used an illegal radio station to appeal directly to illiterate devout women like Pekai, he knew he could successfully convince them to give up basic human rights by making them think that if they questioned him, they were not being devout. Pekai, like many women in Mingora, was a fan of Fazlullah at first. But why would God be displeased by girls' education? And then allow his name to be used by the Taliban to bomb more than four hundred schools? Pekai quickly rejected the broadcast sermons of Fazlullah, but many women around her did not.

When it came to the scarf, Pekai feared the judgment of other women, and she was right to. Women in the community did judge because they saw the men who controlled them judge. It is how social conditioning works.

Pekai stayed veiled, but in her own way, I still consider her to have been the bravest woman in Mingora. Without Pekai, I would not have taken one step forward in my life. Because she was always beside me, encouraging me and encouraging Malala, we felt like we were not alone in our campaign for girls' education. "Malala's activism is my heart's voice," Pekai said. It was two-way. Without me—a husband prepared to see his wife as his equal—as a woman living in a patriarchal society, Pekai, too, could not have begun to feel free.

It is true that Toor Pekai needed my support and my backing, just as so many girls like Malala and women in patriarchal societies need the support of their fathers or husbands for their lives to be different. It is the cultural context of their countries. I think there is nothing wrong with boys and men understanding they have a responsibility to contribute to equality. When men and boys are aware of what women face, when they take measures to make the lives of women and girls easier, it is not patronizing to these women and girls, but rather it is offering much-needed support, based on values of decency and humanity.

In those early days of marriage, our new way of living attracted criticism. And then when Malala was born in July 1997, two years after our stillborn child, and I added her name to the family tree, the first girl for three hundred years, that attracted criticism, too. Some of my distant and closer relatives would not celebrate Malala, or look into her cradle for the fact that she was a girl. This interest—or lack of it—in Malala became a benchmark for me. If Pekai told me somebody had come to visit, I would ask immediately, "Did they want to see Malala?" If they did not, that person was gone for me.

While I did not want to spark a revolution or create a feud, sometimes you have to draw a line between what is acceptable to you and what is unacceptable. Treating Malala with indifference due to her gender? This I could not tolerate.

But God was with us. It was my friend Hidayatullah who noticed that once Malala was born, our fortune with the school changed. It was like she brought with her a rush of good luck. As for me, now with two beautiful females in my life, I was happier than ever before.

It mattered to Pekai as much as it did to me that girls in Mingora whose parents could not afford an education would be given one by the Khushal School. She bitterly regretted her own lack of education, and she did not want to see this repeated in the next generation. Our school was a fee-paying school, but we tried to take in as many girls as possible from families who could not afford it. It was a delicate balance and not always smooth.

By the time Malala and the boys were receiving an education, the Khushal School was just breaking even. I was no longer forced to be the school janitor as well as the school accountant as well as the head teacher. It had grown to eight hundred pupils in three buildings, the original primary school, plus a high school for girls and another high school for boys. I had originally opened one high school, in 2003, but the patriarchal climate of preventing teenage girls from meeting boys made it too difficult for boys and girls to be taught together. I got many complaints from fathers about this and eventually, with regret, I had to separate boys and girls. Hidayatullah and I had also gone our separate ways by then, so I was the overall principal, helped later by Madam Maryam, principal of the girls' school.

Pekai's mission was to get as many girls into the school as possible. This made her a powerful local activist.

Many mothers who saw value in sending their girls to school—even if it was only for a few years—came to Pekai first when they had financial needs, either requesting that Pekai help get their girls into the school for free, or, if they were already there, making the case to her that they could no longer afford the fees. Pekai was a great advocate for these women. Her success was built on the fact that everybody knew I listened to her and often did as she asked. This was very unusual between a husband and wife in our community. Usually, it was the wife who did what the husband asked. Malala later joined Pekai in this lobbying for free places.

Fathers visited me at the school, but their wives knew better. Pekai was visited by women in our home quarters, a collection of small rooms above the school. A scenario might go like this: A mother with children already at the school would say. "Oh, *bhabi,* we cannot pay this fee. It is too much. Please, I beg that you help in reducing it." And Pekai would say, "Okay, I will talk to him." I would come home from teaching and she would say, "Here are the fee cards of the children of this family. Khaista, please bring the bill down for them." And I would say, "Okay, it says here two hundred rupees. So we'll bring it down to one fifty," and then Pekai would haggle. "Too much! It must be a much lower amount!"

The New Year would bring a rush of women to our home because this was the time that extras were added to the fee cards. I was not interested in making money, but I did have to pay the bills and the salaries, and I had to keep Madam Maryam calm, as she was responsible for balancing her own books. Sometimes Madam Maryam would visit me and say, "Sir, Toor Pekai has been admitting new girls again," or "She has been promising that the school will fund their books. My school seems to run half by the 'Toor Pekai Trust.'"

When I confided in Pekai about the need to cover the school's expenses, fearing the school would be lost if I did not, she would say calmly, "God will never let your school go bankrupt if you do this good thing for these girls." She passionately believed it, and it was true. The school never did go bankrupt.

When people think of our family, they think of Malala as one of the world's most powerful activists for social change, because she is. And then after her, perhaps they think of me only because when she was a campaigning child, I was the one who was by her side. We continue to be active together in our girls' education campaign. These days my job is being her father and I am so happy for that. But when I think about Malala and the foundations of her activism, I also think of Toor Pekai. I think of Malala's mother. Toor Pekai's activism is instinctive and spontaneous, built on a fierce moral strength. Her conviction to help others, to be a good person, stems from who she is, where she has come from, and her religious faith. I think we need many more activists like her.

In the early days, Pekai would not have called herself an activist, although she sees herself in that way now. Today, she helps support the families from Pakistan who have come to Birmingham after the Taliban attack on the Army Public School in Peshawar in which 132 children were shot dead along with their 7 teachers. One female teacher was set on fire in front of the children. Pekai is dedicated to supporting two surviving children now living in Birmingham, along with a third boy who is a survivor of another Taliban attack in Pakistan. She tries to make their lives easier with friendship and compassion. I think as human beings our kindness is what distinguishes us from other creatures in the world. We see dogfights and fierce animals tearing each other apart in the jungle, big fish eating smaller fish, but when human beings act with hatred and violence, like the Taliban did, it takes the rest of us to carry on, trying to live in a compassionate, loving way, throwing inhumanity into darkness.

I have since thought about the descriptions others give us, the labels that are used. Often, these labels come from the West. Toor Pekai and I were both "volunteers" before we knew about the concept of "volunteering," a word I learned in America. And as I have said, I only came to know the word "feminist" after living in the UK. For more than forty years, I was living that word but not hearing it.

I do think of Toor Pekai as an early activist. Activism is what? It starts when your actions are about helping others. When Malala and the boys were small, they saw Pekai reaching out beyond our family to people she knew and even to those she did not know. She filled our home with her basic goodness. She was always helping people, feeding them, giving them somewhere to sleep, supporting them, even though she herself did not have much. Helping one person can be as important as motivating an army.

When I look back at those years now and I see how committed

Toor Pekai was to securing an education for other girls like Malala, to helping others, I wonder if I myself should have motivated and helped Pekai to return to the classroom. One of the many questions asked of our family is "How can Malala and her father have been so passionate about education when Toor Pekai was illiterate?" I hope I can do Toor Pekai justice when I answer this question. I have asked Pekai this and she tells me, "I had all the freedoms I wanted. I loved you and I loved my children. I was happy. This was my choice."

In Mingora, it is a sad fact that before the Talibanization, Pekai's lack of formal education did not impact her life. Many women had not received an education. What made Pekai different was that she could exercise her intelligence through her freedom of movement. As a friend once told me, "Toor Pekai might not have an education, but she has an educated mind." And then, following the Talibanization, not even schoolgirls were allowed to go to school, let alone women of Pekai's age.

Like many mothers all over the world, the point in Pekai's life when she felt ready to begin something new came when Atal went to school and there was more time in her day. In 2012, a few months before Malala's attack, Pekai had begun to take lessons in reading and writing English with Miss Ulfat, a teacher at the primary level of the Khushal School.

When the Taliban first started to claim Mingora, Pekai had no experience of standing on a stage, or the confidence to express her ideas about the need to educate girls. Nor did she have Malala's cultural boldness, but what she felt she could not do herself publicly, in front of television cameras or audiences, she was happy for Malala and me to do. We were the people speaking *her* heart and mind, and that is why she gave both of us her great support, never once imagining that the Taliban would come for her child.

WHEN THE BIRDS STOPPED SINGING

Today, once more, blood has been shed in my hometown.
A brother has committed an honour killing.
A brother has killed his sister.
He has followed in the steps of Cain,
who murdered his brother Abel out of jealousy.

Today, once more, society has opposed love.
Custom has opposed love, tradition has opposed love.
Today, once more, jealousy has overcome love.
And lovers are shocked.
Children are afraid.
People flee in terror.

Today, once more, blood has been shed in my hometown
and it has made the universe tremble.
It has made the birds stop singing
as brothers turn the weddings of their sisters into funerals.
Instead of sending them to their new families,
brothers send their sisters to their graves;
instead of following a bride, brothers follow a coffin;
instead of giving a dowry, brothers shed blood;
instead of love, there is killing;
instead of honour, there is shame.

Ziauddin Yousafzai, "Honour Killing," 1994
(tr. by Qasim Swati and Tom Payne)

Twenty-four years have passed since I wrote this poem. It was prompted by a girl and her loved one in Mingora who were killed in front of the girl's house. The murder of women in my community seemed to me to be the ultimate proof of society's callousness towards them, the injustice of their lives. The impact these honor killings had on me as the years went on became even more intense because of how much I loved Toor Pekai and Malala. Such events were not a frequent occurrence, but there were enough of them for me to never allow myself to think they were a thing of the past. Every time an honor killing occurred, my resolve to be a new kind of man deepened.

Toor Pekai and I speak to our friends and relatives in Pakistan every day. Recently, we heard about a woman there who had found love outside her marriage. She had been married for twenty years to an older man, whom she had married when she was a young girl. She had been a replacement for his first wife and a new mother for his children. The woman went missing, and it became clear that she had run away. Her husband's family hunted her down and brought her back to her husband. "Please, spare her. For me, she is clean. There is no shame," he told the male members of the woman's family. Toor Pekai heard about the woman at this point, when she had become her family's shame.

For a brief moment, the woman's future seemed uncertain. Her husband had asked for mercy, but the shame was not just his to dismiss. A meeting of elders was called.

I always say that if Toor Pekai has shed one hundred tears, ninety-five have been for others, not herself. Pekai was distraught. She mounted her own campaign to save the woman's life. From our house in Birmingham, she phoned everybody she could think of who might help to prevent the outcome we feared. "Please do not let them do it," I heard her saying. "They cannot make themselves honorable with this dishonorable thing. Don't do it. It is inhuman. It is not honor."

She asked me to make calls, too, which I did. I contacted somebody I knew who I thought might have some influence. I felt helpless, far away. Had I been there, I would have appealed directly to the family, but I could not do this living in Birmingham. "My hands are tied," my contact told me.

The next day, my phone rang. It was a contact in Pakistan. "It's done," he said. "She was killed last night." The woman was strangled. By the time I took the call, preparations were being made to put her in her grave.

Toor Pekai and I cried for a week. We could not sleep. Apart from the attack on Malala, we have never been so traumatized by anything in our whole lives. I heard that the police in Pakistan made some investigations. But as far as I know, nobody has been brought to justice. Honor killings are against the law in Pakistan, although in the rural areas it is a law that seems to be hardly enforced.

When I define "love," I define it as freedom. The plight of women can be changed if we think differently, if we can break a few norms of family and society, and the governments of such societies abolish discriminatory laws that go against basic human rights. To be clear: it takes courage from both men and women.

Some men feel embarrassed or ashamed to believe in the empowerment of women. There are many men who are prepared to think differently about their daughters' futures, but some men encourage their daughters' freedom without owning the change in themselves. These men believe in equality, and yet they do not shout about it. It needs to be shouted about because misogyny is everywhere still. Sometimes it is in jokes, sometimes it is in subtle casual comments. But it all comes from the same place: a place where women are not seen as equal. When I first came to Britain, a Pakistani taxi driver who was taking me to New Street station in Birmingham wanted to give me some advice:

"Do not trust three things in this country," he said. "The three Ws."

I said, "Okay, what are they?" And he said, "W for weather, W for work, and W for women."

I said to him, "Okay, I may agree with you on two but not three. I mean, yes, I can see that you may get work and lose it. I agree with you on weather because here in the UK, it is raining in the morning and it is sunny in the afternoon. But W for women? This I do not agree with! Tell me faithfully," I said to him. "You are a married person and you have a wife. I ask you who is the most loyal in your family, the most loving in your marriage, you or your wife?" And here he became very embarrassed and laughed nervously. "Yes, you are right. My wife is loyal and loving to our family."

Why did this man who is happy in his marriage tell me this thing about the third W?

"Why say this when you love your own wife, who is a force for good in your family?" I asked him.

"It is just a saying, and people say it!"

And I said to him, "But don't follow! It is man's propaganda, a man's code. Advise against two Ws—work and weather—and one M, man!"

WE CRIED LIKE CHILDREN CRY

The early months and first year or two of our living in the UK were hard for us. Following Malala's attack, we wept more tears than I thought possible. On top of the injuries to her ear and her face, a chunk of her skull had to be taken out and embedded in her stomach while her brain swelled. She now has a metal plate in place of the shattered part of her skull, which in the end could not be used.

When Malala was in the hospital in Birmingham and we were by her side, her beautiful face seemed to be gone. The most shocking and saddening thing was the drooping left side of her face. She had palsy. Our beautiful girl Malala seemed to be a different girl now. She had lost her smile and lost her laughter, and I used to watch Toor Pekai with her and see Pekai's tears roll down her face and splash onto her scarf. Malala's smile would come back later, the next summer following expert surgery, but so many things were unknown at the beginning.

I think trauma can either bring a husband and wife together or force them apart. For us, the trauma of almost losing Malala strengthened our marriage, although almost losing our child made it feel like our lives were truly gone.

We lived first in the hospital hostel and then moved to our apartment on the tenth floor of a city center tower block. We moved twice more after that. In those early days of living in the UK, Toor Pekai would look out of the window and see the women below, so freely walking about the streets in the night air, but dressed in so little by the standards of the women in the bazaars of Mingora. She would weep yet more tears of deep confusion and fear. "Khaista, surely these women will freeze to death."

Where my tears had not fallen at the first news of Malala's attack, now Toor Pekai and I would often cry together the whole night long. We cried like children cry. Our tears were unstoppable. Our bodies shook. It was like the grief was a kind of thunder. There were so many possibilities of how Malala's life might be restricted: paralysis down one side of her face, an inability to speak, limited memory. And yet in the morning we would rise up from the hostel bed and go to Malala lying in her bed for another day filled with a mixture of deep hope and terrible dread that this was the day that would bring more bad news.

Every decision about Malala's well-being Toor Pekai and I made together. Toor Pekai needed me to act as her translator because she could not understand what the British doctors were telling us. Later, Dr. Fiona apologized to me for the fact that she had sought reassurance that I was involving Pekai in the decision making. Many men, she said, do not involve their wives. But for us, there was not one decision made without the other one agreeing, even down to the smallest things such as how to tie back Malala's hair. I honestly do not know what I would have done without Toor Pekai.

With my fear of losing Malala, I felt such guilt, such terrible guilt that I had not stopped her from campaigning. It was Toor Pekai who got me through this period in which I seemed to be stuck in a loop.

I went over my intentions again and again. What had been my aims and goals and objectives? What had I stood for? What had I been working towards that was worth this sacrifice of my child? How could I have miscalculated like this? Why had I not stopped Malala? I had not needed Malala's voice for my own campaign, but I had encouraged her because it was her right to speak if she wanted to. We had stood together, united. But this fight almost left me with the dead body of my child.

Round and round and round my head these thoughts went, during the day and at night.

Toor Pekai was my moral compass. It was she who stopped me from having a full mental collapse. If she had said, "Oh, it is your fault! You put my daughter's life at stake for this higher cause!" how could I have coped with hearing this from the woman closest to me? But I never heard a single word of reproach from Toor Pekai because she instinctively saw the purity of Malala's and my intentions. She had seen the strength of Malala's will. The campaign against the Taliban was not just mine and Malala's, it was Toor Pekai's, too. She had been beside us. In these dark moments after the attack, Pekai reminded me that our fight had been heartfelt. It had been Malala's fight as much as ours. It was God's plan.

People have asked me since, "Does Malala ever say to you, 'Aba, you should have stopped me from speaking'?" And the answer is never. It is a blessing in disguise that Malala remembers nothing of the attack. Six years have passed since then, and I have never once heard a single sigh, a single word, spoken or implied, that somebody else was responsible for what she went through. She does not even speak against the boy who pulled the trigger.

Pekai and I live with the trauma of almost losing Malala every day. It is always there, buried deeper with time but never gone. The pain and fear that come from the possibility of your child dying is felt so deeply that it leaves its scar. All I can try to balance it with is the resolve in my deep love of and thanks to God:

God gave Malala back to us. He brought her life back to us. We hang on to this together. We hang on to this as a family. We are human beings, with a deep commitment to human rights. We believe in what we do and we do what we believe in. It is so simple. It was our family's moral response to a situation we were forced into. I thank God that He was witness to the purity of my intentions.

Pekai has helped me to accept that our family must not blame itself for the fact that the Taliban came at Malala with their guns simply because she wanted to be educated. Malala did not make an army. She did not raise a gun. She raised a voice, which is her right.

Once our life settled down in Birmingham, it was very clear that Pekai's lack of English was impacting everything. She barely knew a word. It was so isolating for her, and she had few Pakistani friends. In Mingora, our house had been full of people. But our house in Birmingham felt empty at the beginning. Once Malala had recovered, the boys and Malala were in school during the day. I would often travel as part of the job I was given as an education attaché to the Pakistani government. And during the holidays, I would travel with Malala, for the Malala Fund that was set up after her attack, or as part of the publicity for Malala's book, *I Am Malala*, or for the documentary film *He Named Me Malala*. I loved this travel with Malala because it was just like it used to be, the two of us together, side by side.

We were so thankful to God that Malala had survived. Pekai would say, "We are here, we are alive, we are together." She would never complain about being left on her own with the boys. But, still, this did not mean she was happy with this new life in the UK. I would hear her often on the phone to a friend in Swat saying, "Why am I not educated? Why is my life difficult? I don't understand anything." Sometimes I would see her wandering around the garden with the leftovers from our dinner. With nobody in the community to feed, she would leave our food for the birds, but the birds knew not to eat it.

One of the earliest English phrases Pekai learned to say was "top up," because it enabled her to buy a top-up card for her mobile phone, which then meant she could ring friends and relations in Pakistan. We all missed Pakistan, but for Pekai, there were many basic elements of UK life to master, like transport and calendars, that the rest of us found much easier. She did not know how to spell her name in English. When she had to fill in forms she had no idea when her birthday was. On top of general day-to-day confusion, Pekai suffered terrible headaches that the doctor said were a reaction to the trauma of the attack on Malala.

Despite the headaches, Pekai enrolled herself in an ESOL (English for Speakers of Other Languages) course. I would do my best to translate for Pekai, and Malala would, too, but we were not always with her. When shopping was needed, we'd try to go together. I realized sadly that her life in the UK, in the beginning, was a complete reversal of the independence she had had in Pakistan. Pekai could not be free in Birmingham in the beginning because of the language barrier, and because of her fear.

Key to Toor Pekai's proper education has been her tutor, Janet Culley-Tucker. She met Janet first at the ESOL class, but initially these classes were too much for Pekai. Her headaches were too painful. Still, she remained in touch with Janet, and a few months later, her lessons resumed but in our house instead.

Janet still comes to the house to teach Pekai, not in a professional capacity but more as a friend. Pekai remains very protective of her time with Janet. Sometimes she takes Janet upstairs to our bedroom, where they can work undisturbed by the noise of the house. It was Janet who first taught Pekai how to read and write the word "education."

Janet saw from the beginning that Pekai, like the rest of us Yousafzais, was extremely competitive. She *wanted* to learn. Slowly, Pekai's confidence started to return. Now, she often has her books with her, and she will ask anybody who comes to the house if they will help her in conversation. The fierce determination had never really left her. It was just that a new life had challenged it.

Janet assigned Pekai homework based on the idea of "language experience," a teaching technique that is built on trying to relate as much of the language as possible to the life of the student. Pekai always completed these assignments to a high standard, but I would see that in her homework Malala was described as "a 17-year-old student" and the information about the boys was limited to their favorite fruits, colors, and hobbies.

Such descriptions were impressive in how accurate the vocabulary and grammar were, but they were a fraction of what had happened to us, and it made me acutely aware of the difficult journey my wife was on, living in a country in which she could not speak the language. She could not convey to anybody other than us the complex thoughts in her head and the emotions in her heart. Many adult learners in Birmingham are first-generation immigrants who have given birth to their children in the UK. These children are British and yet their mothers are still learning how to read and write their own names and the names of their children in English. Pekai's determination to succeed was yet another way she made me proud of her.

In Pakistan there is a brilliant man called Rafiullah Kakar who went to Oxford on a Rhodes scholarship. He started a campaign, #WeRejectPatriarchy, aimed at men, encouraging them to write, "My name is...My wife's name is..." Rafiullah Kakar started the campaign after he celebrated his own partner's success by revealing her name and Facebook ID. In addition to the comments of support he received, there were messages of criticism and others advising caution about naming his partner. In response to the criticism, he launched the campaign and wrote, "It is a shame that in 21st century we, especially Pashtun and Baloch men, can't even disclose the names of women of our family let alone empowering them. We are at least 500 years behind the civilised world. What I experienced is the story of every other Pashtun and Baloch male who is trying to change the status quo."

It was so moving reading some of the comments that followed this post supporting #WeRejectPatriarchy. My own post, written with great pride, went like this:

I am Ziauddin Yousafzai. I am a proud husband of Toor Pekai Yousafzai. Toor Pekai is a housewife and a student. #WeRejectPatriarchy.

Not long ago, Pekai and I were in a supermarket doing some grocery shopping. I was pushing the cart while Pekai was loading the food. When we came to the checkout, I joined a line. I felt a tap on my shoulder. It was Pekai.

"You are in the wrong queue," she said.

"Why? I'm here to pay," I said.

She shook her head and pointed to the sign that read "Basket."

She looked pleased. "You have a trolley, not a basket. You need to be in the trolley queue."

It was such a small thing and yet it symbolized so much. I hugged her tightly and said, "Pekai, you make me so happy. I never stop being proud of you."

Oh my goodness, Toor Pekai likes to shop. I think I might owe the shops of Birmingham's Bullring a debt of gratitude for helping Pekai begin to feel more at home in the UK. I will admit that after six years in the UK, I get into such a muddle with what I must wear. If I have to attend meetings or functions, there is often dress advice: smart, smart casual, business suit, formal suit, evening dress. What are all these things? In Pakistan, I wore a simple shalwar kamiz, but here Pekai tells me that my trousers must match my sweater and that on some occasions I must wear smart trousers and a shirt but no tie, but definitely a smart jacket, and then the color and pattern of my shirt must match my trousers. This color matching is impossible, and Pekai is always on hand with an opinion! But truly Pekai loves new clothing dilemmas because they present her with another opportunity to go shopping.

Toor Pekai has such an extreme love of shopping, mostly of dresses and bags and shoes, that we all love to tease her about it. I believe that Toor Pekai would be happy shopping every day, all day long, going up and down the escalators on the Bullring as happy as a person could ever be. I cannot manage ten minutes of this with her. Sometimes, we seem to go up and down, up and down, and I say, "Oh, Pekai, please! I just need a cup of tea." Recently, a friend said to me, "But Zia, does Pekai not get tired out after such a long day on her feet?" And I said, "Tired? You must be joking. If Pekai shopped constantly for five days, on the fifth day she would be as fresh as a person who has just taken a shower. She goes shopping to feel fresh. She will never feel worn-out."

But, really, I find this trait in Pekai so lovely. She is so generous and enthusiastic about her shopping trips. I think perhaps it is a sign that she belongs here finally and that her English is good enough now. She is as free as she was in the bazaars of Mingora, and like then, she is no happier than when she is shopping for other people whom she feels she can help. It proves to me, too, that you can be perfect companions even if some of your interests are poles apart. I hate shopping—hate it—but I love Toor Pekai.

Being Malala's mother has changed Toor Pekai's life, not only because we no longer live in our homeland. Malala is a global figure, and as a result occasionally Pekai is placed in the limelight, too. She has learned, with time, that rather than allowing these public appearances to present her with the dilemma of how much she should cover her face with her scarf, she can put her position as the mother of Malala to some use. She is happy in front of the camera these days—her scarf always covers her hair but no longer her face—and she will agree to be interviewed by journalists and take part in discussion panels with the help of an interpreter. This would have been unthinkable for her five years ago. As a result, I think that Pekai is becoming very influential among ordinary women in our homeland. These women might now think of Malala as they might once have thought of Benazir Bhutto, a member of the educated elite, even though Malala is not from the elite class. But in Pekai they see a woman with no formal schooling from a village in northern Pakistan who has brought up a daughter to achieve all she dreamed of. When Pekai speaks, these women hear the voice of a woman like them, an ordinary woman speaking for herself, claiming rights for herself and her daughter.

When Pekai was small, she played a game with her cousins in which they predicted their futures. One of the girls imagined she would be married to a widower, a mother to his children and her own, cooking and cleaning for a big family. The second girl saw a lonely life ahead, but when it came to Pekai, she said, "I dream to be in a town, not here in Shangla, and grills and roti will be brought to me from the bazaar. I'd really enjoy that."

To some extent, the girls predicted their own futures. The friend who predicted a big family has many children, the other one is a single mother with a son, and Pekai leads a different kind of life altogether. Back then, she knew she wanted something more than the usual fate of girls in Karshat, but her dreams were limited. I liked so much bringing Pekai ready-made food and kebabs in Mingora because it pleased me that she had not been in the kitchen herself. I still do bring roti and kebabs from the local Pakistani restaurant in Birmingham. This amuses her. But she does not want grills and roti for the next generation. What she wants for girls in Shangla is that they will say: "I want to be an engineer" or "I want to be a doctor" or "I want to run my own social enterprise." This is the aim and it is possible with education. We know this because Malala is proof.

Every year, on the anniversary of the attack, Pekai gives Malala a birthday card as a mark of her second life, given to us by God. When Malala was fighting for her life, Pekai prayed so hard outside the hospital that my nephew asked her to lower her voice, but she had confidence in her loud prayer to God.

Pekai believes that when your heart is full of genuine love for humanity, then this heart full of love and kindness and compassion will please the bigger, higher universal creator—for her, it is God. As a result, God's heart will be filled with even more love and kindness for you. It is the gracious cycle of goodness. This is the essence of Toor Pekai.

Recently, we had very bad thunderstorms in Birmingham. Pekai was with Janet working on her English. Janet could see that Pekai was nervous and anxious. "Come on, Pekai," she said. "We'll watch a film instead." She thought the film would be a nice distraction. But Pekai looked horrified. "No film," she told her. When I returned, Toor Pekai told me what had happened. For Pekai, the thunder meant God was displeased. Watching a film, she thought, would have made God even more cross. "Oh, Pekai," I said, "you must not worry about displeasing God by watching a film."

We laughed about it. But Pekai loves God. She never ever forgets that God gave her back her daughter.

Daughter

because we, too, can be brave enough
to break the chains that enslave us.
We, too, will think afresh.

Ziauddin Yousafzai, from "I Promise," 1988
(tr. by Qasim Swati and Tom Payne)

A STAR RISES

W<small>HEN</small> M<small>ALALA WAS BORN</small>, it was very early in the morning. Her birth brought a light to my life like the brightest star rising in the sky. She was a morning star in our lives. I could hear the call for morning prayer in the background as the neighbor who had helped Pekai knocked urgently on my door. I had been sleeping on the sofa of my office in the school that night so that I was separate from Pekai. She gave birth to Malala in small, simple quarters. Men never attended their wives during labor.

But as that prayer call sounded over the rooftops and Mingora began to wake up, I opened the door to be told, "You have a daughter in your home, a newborn child, a girl child." And I ran to Pekai and to my daughter and they were lying together in the cot bed. And believe me when I say, I saw the glitter and the shine in my girl child's eyes. Her eyes were wide-open and bright, not pressed shut, and I saw them shine. Twenty years on, I am still in the aura of that light. I'm still in the happiness of that moment. She was so pure and so refined, her face was so clear, it was as if she had been alive a month rather than having just endured the rigor of birth. I felt I was the most blessed man for having a daughter, a daughter like Malala. I took her in my arms and I could not stop looking at her, this glittering baby. This was the moment, the moment when I looked down at her, into her open eyes, and I knew that this was the start of a journey, her journey and mine, together.

When I saw her, I felt she was the baby I had been waiting for. It is fair to ask: why should I want to bring a girl into a world, into a patriarchal society, that was not set up to support her? But the answer is simple. When I thought about being a father to a daughter, I imagined my role as completely different from the fathers I had seen around me when I was a son with sisters, when I myself was a boy with no girls in my class. I knew what kind of father I was going to be if I was ever lucky enough to have a daughter. I was completely clear about it. I was going to be a father who believed in equality, and believed in a girl as she grows into a woman, and who raises her so that she believes in herself, so that in her life she can be free as a bird.

I had helped women before Malala's birth. I had stood beside my cousin in support of her, and I had spent a lot of time thinking about my sisters, wishing I could do more to improve their lives. But really and truly, the first person in my life with whom I was able to start this journey of equality was Malala. My own real *active* journey begins with her, because, as I have said, change starts with you. Malala was new and did not need to be shackled to the past. With her birth, I could see the potential of what the world offered with new eyes. My baby became like a touchstone for me.

I was not worried that my society would cut down this child. As I looked at her, lying in her secondhand cradle, I believed that she could do anything in the world, this beautiful child, and because I had faith in her, that was enough.

But it is also true that I needed faith in my own position as her father. I had such instinctive, powerful love that I felt as long as I was beside her, supporting her, nothing could stand in her way. I look back and I see myself resolved and determined that these social norms I lived with, these traditions full of misogyny and male chauvinism, would not cut her down. I was her shield.

I said to myself, "Ziauddin, people will have to yield to you, to support you in this journey, because you will never let them pressure you to fall back into the old ways." I was strong enough that I believed in the change that had started in my heart. I believed that this change itself was so powerful and important and just and fair and truthful that no power on earth could move me from it. Not only was Malala a girl child but she was also my *first living* child. I believe that had Malala been my third child or my fourth child after a line of sons, I would still have felt this sense of purpose for her, but there is something unique about a first-born child, especially because we had lost her sister.

There is a curious thing that happens in Pakistan. Some women are celebrated by patriarchal men, like the late Benazir Bhutto, daughter of Zulfikar Ali Bhutto and Maryam Nawaz Sharif, daughter of three-time prime minister Nawaz Sharif. But these women are of the elite class. These elite women are admired by common people; they are celebrated by highborn men and common men. These men join the political parties of these great women, and they respect them. But their own daughters, lowborn girls living in rooms without servants and placed in secondhand cradles, are not believed in. The men lose faith in their own kin. This is a class struggle in Pakistan as well as a struggle for equality. I ask these men, "If you accept Benazir Bhutto as Benazir Bhutto, why can't you accept ordinary girls like Lubna,

Kalsoom, and Saba? Why can't you dream for ordinary girls in your own home? You have these great women right beside you, sitting at your fireplace."

Both Malala and Toor Pekai are viewed differently now. As I have said, women in our old communities look at Pekai as a role model today, because of the way her status as Malala's mother has given her the freedom to start speaking in public. Because of Malala's global profile and her Nobel Peace Prize, they regard us as a different social class, but we are not. I have said to all our family members, "We are from you, we are with you, and we are among you." One of Pekai's male cousins said to her, "Toor Pekai, you are amazing. Speak up. Whenever you speak, you are always so brilliant and we are proud of you." He said this to Pekai but makes no attempt to encourage his own wife to come forward. I have often said to men in my own community, "Why should you only acknowledge and recognize women once they stand before you on a public stage? Why should you not accept all women as human beings like yourself? Why must you wait for a school to be burned and a brave girl to rise up and say, "Why are you burning my school?" And then she becomes Malala of Pakistan? Why should one girl be targeted with a bullet and then she becomes Malala globally? Let a girl like Malala be Malala without this sacrifice!

Why do ordinary men think their daughters are not good enough to be leaders? It is as if these big powers, big jobs, big titles are just meant first for men and then for empowered rich women. This was not how I saw it for Malala and her future. Because if a parent does not give a child the space to think anything in life is possible, it is an uphill struggle for the child to believe in her own potential.

When I looked at Malala asleep in her bed, I did not think, "Yes, she is Malala and I love her, but Ziauddin, be realistic, we don't have much money and she is a lower-class girl."

Never. Never. I believed in anything and everything for her. Instead of writing her off, or limiting her with established prejudices, I thought instead, "She will change the world! She will move mountains! If she is given the chance, this girl can go up and she can move the world for everyone. She is meant for the stars."

I say the same thing to all fathers, brothers, men, and boys today: The world will not come to you, inside your home, and introduce your daughter or your sister to you, when she is still a child, as the next great woman, the next great scientist or politician, the next Malala. It is up to you as a father or a brother, and a mother, to be the first to accept and encourage potential in the girl you love. It is up to you to recognize her and to believe in her, to believe that, yes, this small child in her crib can grow up to be these things. If you do not say that your children are the best or that they can work towards their dreams, then who will? And our children need it, believe me, they need it.

It is well known that I named Malala after Malalai of Maiwand, the female Pashtun fighter who died on the battlefield for her cause. Of course, I did not name her Malala for the warfare or the battle or the martyred death. I named her this because she was the first woman in our culture who had her own identity, her own name. I remember the first time I properly contemplated what the story meant, before Malala was born. I had been sitting in my friend's house in Mingora, long before I was married. My friend Usman Olasyar would often feed me to help my plight. I was engaged to Pekai, who was back in Shangla, waiting for me to earn enough so that we could get married. I was sitting on his daybed drinking chai and looking at a framed poster of a girl on a horse, a girl who was drawn in all her grandeur and glory. Around her were the famous words "Thousands of men might have reached to the zenith of their success, but they are no match for what Malalai of Maiwand did with a single call." I was so moved. One call of this girl Malalai of Maiwand is far more excellent than thousands of men of excellence. I found it so romantic. And I found it so just that I thought, "If I am lucky enough to have a daughter, I will name her Malala."

When Malala was very small and she talked of wanting to be the prime minister, I would see people smirk. Their look said it: "You? The prime minister of Pakistan?" From the beginning, I thought, "Well, this shining morning star, she might just be smarter than the one already at the top."

So when people laughed at her dreams, it brought out the same anger in me that I had felt when male members of my family had shown no interest as she lay in her cradle, just because she was a girl.

Still, in order for this hope I had for Malala to blossom, to thrive and grow instead of dying like a neglected, thirsty plant, there had to be an extra ingredient: education. I am a romantic and an idealist, but in this I saw an urgent, practical need. Just as education had taken me from Shangla, my daughter's only way out of the confines of our society would be through gaining a degree and a job.

Even the rich girls needed an education. The rich boys, sons of feudal lords, might rise up through money and family power, but education for any girl in Pakistan, and so many countries, is the only way out of patriarchy and early marriage.

MALALA'S SCARF

Malala was admitted to the nursery school class of my school when she was five years old. She loved everything about being there. The desks, the books, the uniform. As she grew older, she used to linger there with the other girls, unwilling to leave. Because we lived in two rooms above the classrooms, she had been coming in and out from the moment she could walk, but the moment she became a student herself was of huge significance.

We had three terms a year, and from the beginning, I bought her a folder and she used to keep her answer sheets clipped there in order, along with each test, the checked papers, and certificates. We have some of them even now. It was as if she knew that this life in the classroom was precious. She wanted to treasure every bit of it, respect every bit of it, give it the small honor of neatness and order. It was an intense kind of treasuring, a kind of mad love, a desperate love. Really, it was an obsession with school.

The girls wore a uniform, which was a white shalwar and a dark blue kamiz, with a white scarf in summer and a black scarf in winter. Their shoes and socks were black. Malala carried a bright pink rucksack with a darker pink trim.

Sometimes I would come home from teaching and find Malala crouched down by the open tap in a small concrete antechamber off of our living quarters. It was our only source of water and it was where the dishes and clothes were washed, not every day for the clothes, but three or four times a week. Malala was often beside the tap, barely taller than where it came out from the wall, and in her hand would be her school scarf. She would have the scarf in a bucket resting on the table below the tap and be pushing and pulling and squeezing it, rinsing away the dust and grime collected through her daily carefree life in Mingora.

Malala took such care in this. She washed her school socks, too. She was such a helpful girl to Pekai. Everywhere in Mingora dust hung in the air, from the traffic and the heat. Malala did not like dirt, but I like to think of this scarf washing as an example of her pride in being a schoolgirl. She scrubbed it until the water was murky brown, and then she wrung it out and clipped it on our washing line on the roof. The sun dried it almost instantly, and the next day it was on her head, clean and fresh, ready for another day at her school desk.

Was Malala's passion for school due to nature or nurture? I think both. You can say that Malala was a perfect seed in the perfect soil, a magical seed in the most conducive soil for its nourishment. Our home was devoted to learning and she was devoted to learning. But she was also the luckiest girl as well, compared with some of her friends, because she had us supporting her, too. Education is not just about learning facts and sitting exams. The best schools are where all students' potentials are unlocked, where all girls are given the wings to fly, and where they have this confidence built up in them to live a successful life of their own making.

When I started the high school in 2003, I knew that giving girls power inside themselves was equally as important as teaching them English and Urdu. I would walk around the classrooms, and sometimes the girls would talk to me about how they wanted to learn but were getting no support at home from their parents. I would often mediate with these parents, but it was hard changing the old, ingrained view that a girl's education beyond a certain point was a waste of time. In Mingora, going to school at a young age was not unusual. It was when the girls became teenagers that they disappeared from the classroom, as most often their families prepared them for marriage.

In the beginning, before even Malala and the boys were in school, we were not a privileged family. We did not have lots of money or a big bungalow. But we did have one another. Our family was a very close and loving family, and it gave us strength. It was not like at that stage I had physically taken this gun and was saying to all men, "Okay! I will fight with anyone who opposes Malala. I will oppose anyone who gets in my daughter's way." That kind of defiance came when the Taliban invaded. Before that, it was a kind of spiritual strength; people felt our adoration and affection for her.

Pekai wanted so much for Malala to have the education she had not had. The only area where they differed was how much Malala should cover herself in public. Many women walked around our bazaars in burkas, triangles of thick cloth that fitted their heads tightly like caps and then flowed right down to the floor, covering every inch of the body to protect their honor. It takes skill to wear a garment like this because walking requires managing the burka flapping around your feet. But once mastered, the burka provides a window through which its wearer can view the world without being seen by eyes other than those of her husband. Pekai did not wear a burka but as I have said, she covered her face with a scarf. Malala wore a scarf but exposed her face. Malala refused to comply when Pekai asked her to cover more of her face. She did not want to view the world from behind a veil. She wanted to see it with an open face, just like the men did. I agreed with her, to be honest. I saw no shame in this. Not only would Malala not cover her face, but she would stare straight back at any man who looked at her. Sometimes, while out with Pekai, she would pass men and would look back at them and catch them staring at other veiled women, walking with their eyes fixed to the floor. "Malala, please," Pekai would say. "Malala! What are you doing? Look away. Do not look at these men." But Malala would reply, "Well, if they can stare at me, why can't I stare back?"

Malala thought of it as a sort of "staring problem," but she was fearless and curious about these public boundaries that felt wrong to her. She was, even then, claiming a right she saw as her own.

WHEN THE TALIBAN STOLE OUR KOH-I-NOOR

Whatever Malala is, whatever Malala has, it is because of her education. If Malala had not been a fifth, sixth, or seventh grader, if she herself had not had this love of learning, if she had not been inquiring and bold and confident inside the home and out, she would never have become a powerful voice for girls all over the world. "Malala," the girl who became a role model, without her education would have remained her whole life unsung, unheard. Her astounding voice, which is heard all over the world, would have been silent.

I knew and she knew that an education was the only way out for her, the only chance she had to make a future for herself, to be financially independent, to make everything for her life that she alone decided.

For Malala, education was the Koh-i-noor in her life. The

Koh-i-noor is a diamond that has had a long and dramatic journey from India to Britain, where it is now part of the crown jewels. Qualifications were Malala's Koh-i-noor. There was not a Plan B. None. If not an education and then a career, for a girl like Malala there would have been a husband by the time she was twenty—sixteen if she was unlucky. On a different path with no education, Malala would be the mother of two children by now, not an Oxford-educated Nobel laureate.

Whenever anybody has asked me how Malala became who she is, I have often used the response "Ask me not what I did but what I did not do. I did not clip her wings." In Pakistan I occasionally came across families who kept a bird, perhaps a dove, in their courtyard, and this bird was no longer able to fly. It would waddle around the dusty floor, lifting its head and moving it from one side to the other, but the vital ingredient in its life was gone. Somebody, no doubt a father or a brother, had taken some scissors to its primary feathers and clipped them so short that flight was no longer possible. It was a kind of act of ownership over that poor defenseless creature, for entertainment or the desire to have an obedient pet, forced to live against its primal instinct of flight. It always struck me as cruel.

When I say of Malala "I did not clip her wings," what I mean is that when she was small, I broke the scissors used by society to clip girls' wings. I did not let those scissors near Malala. I wanted to let her fly high in the sky, not scratch around in a dusty courtyard, grounded by social norms, and I would stand by her, protecting her, until she had the confidence and strength to fly high herself, no longer in need of protection.

How do you build a child, girl or boy, to be fearless and confident? I think you do it by praise. What I did every day, for the boys, too, but for Malala especially, if she did a small or big thing as a child, if she had some good grades or she came to me with a nice piece of homework or she expressed a new beautiful, innocent idea, I praised her. I loved her creativity. I endeavored to make her feel like she was the wisest human being ever to come to this earth, like she was the most beautiful human being to have ever existed. And this, I think, is the responsibility of every parent with their daughters and with their sons. All parents can nurture their children in this way. I see around me so many children who are brought up in ways that are not focused on the child at all. In the East and West, we teach our children that they must believe in God, the prophets, saints, and the holy books.

We tell them to believe in angels that they cannot see and, in the East, *jin,* the creature that came before us. But our children are here in front of us, with all their whole physical bodies, full of passions and emotions, with their sentiments and their wisdom and their brains. They exist with everything they have, but we rarely tell them to believe in themselves.

As Malala got older, her confidence in public speaking grew. She would stand up on a stage in debating and speaking competitions and display the same charisma and confidence that the world has seen in her since. She used to take part in all of the regular competitions, and she did so well in them. Before the Taliban came, she became the first ever Speaker of the Child Assembly in Swat, a position she won through an election. Both girls and boys together made up this assembly, and there were many schools from all over Swat taking part.

Malala's class was a unique and clever class. Every girl in it was competitive, but in a good way. There was no jealousy among them; it was more that they were all united in this journey to be educated. They were all smart, but some of them met with resistance from the men in their families.

Once, when I decided to hold a joint debating competition between the boys' and the girls' divisions of my school, in the boys' building, a girl's brother came to find me. "Sir, my sister will not go to the boys' school and she will not speak in front of the boys. Why have you suggested that the girls will be speaking before them with an uncovered face?"

These were the so-called taboos that I often had to deal with. If their parents had allowed them, I believe at least ten girls in that class could have grown up to have the influence Malala has. In peacetime, everything about our lives was proactive, about working towards a better life. Malala was always speaking in competitions, and she was making a name for herself on the school circuit. But she was a young girl and it was really just a hobby she was good at, a source of trophies and medals and another way in which she could feel listened to and appreciated and valued. It is ironic to think that just as Pekai and I were encouraging these things that built up her self-esteem, Malala was about to lose the most fundamental part of her life.

My activism had always been proactive. I wanted improvement in our community. I wanted more democracy, more planting of trees, cleaner water, more schools. I wanted better living conditions for everybody in Mingora. As a head teacher, every day I came up against patriarchal fathers who did not want to educate their daughters, but I never once thought that educating a girl would be banned.

When militant Talibanization started in the Swat Valley in 2007, I was like a man who had had the earth dragged away from under his feet. Where is a man left when this happens to him? He is nowhere. By banning girls' education, the Taliban was taking away Malala's future. The Koh-i-noor had been snatched from us. All those dreams and hopes of a better life that I had had for Malala since her birth, and for the girls in the Khushal School and the 50,000 schoolgirls in the Swat Valley, were disappearing.

The Taliban marched through Mingora regularly with flags in their hands and guns strapped to their backs. There were Taliban everywhere. Men who had once been normal people in our community were now part of this violent army. Often they came through the streets in jeeps, the wheels skidding and kicking up dust. Their hair was long and dirty under their turbans, and their trousers were tucked into their socks. They wore trainers on their feet. They swarmed around the women's markets, their eyes darting around looking for women who they felt were not subservient enough. Every morning and every night, there would be stories on the news and in the newspapers that another three schools had been bombed, four schools bombed. More than four hundred schools were destroyed in all, and it became routine that every day a school would be blown apart. And then came the ban on girls' education, on January 15, 2009.

I had broken into pieces the scissors that would have clipped Malala's wings. I had raised her to believe that she could fly as high as she wanted, but the Taliban came armed not with scissors to ground her but with bombs and guns. After the sermons on the illegal radio station, the violence became inhumane. People I knew who opposed the Taliban were taken away in the night and found in the morning, beheaded in the square or thrown in the sewer.

The idea of not standing up to them, of keeping quiet, was not an option for me. It was instinctive. I had no choice because I believe that human life does not mean breathing out carbon dioxide and taking in oxygen. I believe that human life means humanity, with all its dignity, with all the basic human rights we are entitled to. I will not live for one day, not one day, without fighting for these principles. If I could live for just one day according to my own choices versus hundreds of years in subjugation to bigots and murderers, I would choose one day of freedom.

Of course I felt fear, but fear also gives you courage. I feared I would be killed, because many people were being murdered, but my bigger fear was that Malala and all the girls of the land would be without education, that girls born in our part of Pakistan would have a dark future. I was acting upon an unshakable conviction about a girl's right to be educated, but it was also a panic, a terror of what might become of Malala's future and the future of Pakistan.

Over time, there were very few people prepared to speak out. They would say, "We cannot speak on it because our lives are very dear to us. We will not speak because we are frightened." And if somebody did speak? Sometimes they would say what the Talibs wanted to hear: "We demand that Islam and Sharia be implemented in Swat, then there will be peace!"

And I would stand up and oppose them: "This is not about Islam!" I would tell whoever wanted to listen. "We do not have any un-Islamic things in Swat. We are already an Islamic society. This is about power! This is about greedy people. It is about thugs who want to come in and control our lives. This is unacceptable! Indeed, this hatred and violence is un-Islamic!"

As people around me became silent, I spoke more. I shouted my message over the squares of Mingora. I tried to make everything I said simple and logical, so that everybody could understand. The journalists who were covering the conflict liked this quality.

The way I saw it was that I was playing my role in the future of a country. Standing up to the Taliban was the responsibility I took for our future generations. It was not just Malala's dreams and rights I was protecting. It was the dreams and rights of all the girls in my school and in the beautiful valley of Swat. My pain and my anger was for my daughter and all the daughters of this country. I was running a school for girls. There were 50,000 other girls who were in school in Swat. What did this Talibanization mean? It meant no women in power; it meant no free women, no girls' education. It meant women would be slaves.

I was so devastated when I contemplated Malala's future in these terms. Can you imagine how that felt after everything I had tried to do for her? The pain felt almost physical.

Because of the way in which I spoke, I was often approached by journalists for quotes and information. One of the journalists covering the conflict was Abdul Hai Kakar, my friend who worked for BBC Urdu and for whom Malala started writing her secret diary under the pen name Gul Makai later in that year of 2009. Abdul Hai Kakar warned me that I was becoming too prominent. "Zia," he said, "you are speaking too often. Danger will come. I have told my office that we must stop using your name and your voice so much."

Journalists in the area were both under surveillance from the Pakistani army and at the same time receiving threats from the Taliban. "We will see you!" the Taliban commanders would say, which was how a death threat was spoken.

"We are all walking dead bodies, Zia," Abdul Hai Kakar warned me. "We are carrying our funeral on our shoulders." But he did not stop reporting despite these threats and neither did I stop speaking.

Nobody wants to die. Human life is precious. I didn't want to die, but I knew that what I was doing might cost me my life. I started receiving death threats, pushed under the door and through the media. It is traumatic to think about your death, about leaving your small children on their own, bringing them into this world and then leaving it early. The most fearful thing for me was not that the Taliban was going to finish my life but that I would be leaving my children without a father. But at the same time, I thought, "I am on the right path. I am raising my voice for the very basic human rights, for education and peace in my country. And, God forbid, God forbid it ever happens, but if it does, I will not be repenting it." Friends were often telling me to go carefully. Toor Pekai was terrified and would open the door herself, assuming that the Taliban would never kill a woman. Malala was terrified for me, too, but neither of them urged me to stop.

One friend said to me, "You have already received a death threat, Ziauddin. The way you are speaking, it will be fatal. You are inviting death." And I remember what I told him. I said, "Right now, my happiness is the love I have for my family, my children, and my wife. But if I die? My mother and father will be there waiting for me. I will be going back to this first family." This is how I justified my own activism to myself. I saw myself in a bigger picture. I saw my activism not as a large noble thing that would change the world but as something I could do for my community. And ultimately, I thought, "If I die? It's worth it because protecting my rights or the rights of the people of my community is worth my life." I received death threats in 2008 and in 2009, but the Taliban did not take my life. I did not stop my activism with these threats, although I took precautions such as changing my routine. But when ten months before Malala was attacked in 2012 there was a threat on her life? This was my Achilles' heel. The Taliban had found a way of silencing me.

A BRAVE BIRD

There is a general view, I think, that Malala was attacked just for going to school, or because she broke the ban on girls' education in January 2009. We did break the ban on girls' education then. For those who wanted to, we pretended the girls in the higher grades were in grade four, the cutoff, and then later we held their classes in secret. But Malala was shot by the Taliban because of the power of her voice. It had started to make a real difference in Pakistan. It had grown louder and more powerful between 2009 and 2012. The people of our country were listening to her. Malala's voice was so much more powerful than my own voice because it was coming from a child's heart. She was not political; she was innocent. She just believed in education. Her intentions were so pure. What had been a talent for debate on the school circuit grew into something much bigger. Never once did we think that the Taliban would attack a child. They had never attacked any child before.

The army had cleared the Taliban from Mingora in 2009 after a short period in which we fled as IDPs (internally displaced persons). Pekai took the children to Shangla while I stayed in Peshawar to campaign with my friends Fazal Maula, Ahmad Shah, and Muhammad Farooq.

When we returned to Mingora later that year, our city was like a ghost town. Our school, where the security forces had stayed, was covered in graffiti and rubbish, and the furniture was a mess. Malala and I continued to speak publicly about girls' rights to education. In our minds, it was not fear we felt but great pride that Malala was raising her voice and speaking for the people of our country. As her voice grew louder and was heard all over the country, wherever she went, people would gather around her. At airports, people would ask for her autograph or her photograph. This support was huge, and if you are supported by your people, everything else becomes small. Those who could not raise their own voices were who mattered to her. She was *their* voice. Pekai said to both of us: "If you do not speak out, who else will?"

When I cast my mind back to those days, Malala's activism together with mine, I see that we were both so busy in that fight. In Swat, this fight was not a solo fight. I was a member of the council of elders in Swat and I was the president of the Global Peace Council, which meant there were other men who were campaigning, too. Some of my close peace activist friends were killed in terrorist attacks and others were injured. There had been other girls in my school who had spoken out, but this stopped over time as their fathers had become scared.

When you are in the battle, you hardly think about other things, about what is happening around you. You are focused on the battle. For a very long time, I did not think about the threat to Malala's life at all. This is because I took it for granted that she would be safe and nothing in the world would ever happen to her, a teenage girl. It is why I allowed her to keep the anonymous diary under the name of Gul Makai. I did not think she was at risk.

And when we both took part in a *New York Times* documentary that year called *Class Dismissed*, I did not imagine that placed her at risk, either. I suppose I thought, "Yes, the Taliban has destroyed more than four hundred schools, but they have never attacked a child. Why would they do it? And a girl? How could they come after a girl?" I took her safety for granted, which I see now as a kind of naïveté.

People who criticize Toor Pekai and me for allowing Malala to become a child activist in such a dangerous place have a right to do that. Of course, I know that people think, "You are an idealist. Your first priority should be your life," but we are all human beings. We are alike in many things, but we are different in many things as well. The way I saw it was that our response was like the instinctive courage of a mother bird. When a bird sees its chicks in danger, when she sees a snake wrapping itself around her nest, she flies up and she cries. She chirps and shouts in her own language. She does not do nothing. She does not go and hide somewhere else in the forest.

Our whole family had lived in such a way that accepting Talibanization was impossible. We had read and believed in the words of Martin Luther King Jr., of Gandhi, of Nelson Mandela and Bacha Khan, people who had shown real bravery during great struggles. So I would not compromise. And Malala was the same. She was a born activist, and circumstances gave her a platform. You can't "make" a Malala. You can't "make" a Martin Luther King Jr. or a Rosa Parks. As a parent, all you can do is inspire them by your actions, by your own values. As

Malala's platform grew in Pakistan, Toor Pekai and I could see that Malala was not an ordinary girl, or rather that she was an ordinary girl but with extraordinary courage, talent, and wisdom. I used to tell her, "Jani, your speeches go to the core of people's hearts."

Two key moments of recognition of Malala's influence in Pakistan came at the end of 2011. The first was that she was nominated for the International Children's Peace Prize by Archbishop Desmond Tutu. The citation read, "Malala dared to stand up for herself and the other girls and use national and international media to let the world know girls should have the right to go to school." She did not win this prize, but we were so proud. She would win it two years later, after the attack. However, at the end of 2011, Pakistan's prime minister, Yousaf Raza Gilani, decided to honor her bravery with our country's first National Youth Peace Prize. The award was later named after her and became known as the National Malala Peace Prize. As a result of this, at Malala's request, the prime minister directed the authorities to set up an IT campus in the Swat Degree College for Women.

Malala was already beginning to think about setting up her own organization to help poor girls go to school. Even then, aged fourteen, she had big ambitions. Her profile in Pakistan as a child activist was well established.

Pakistan is a country full of conspiracies. Dissenters said Malala's fight was really mine, that her voice was my voice. But if I had wanted to make Malala my extension, part of me, part of my "campaign," I think she would have remained very small. She would not have grown bigger than me in terms of her impact. She would not have completely overshadowed me. The way she was able to communicate was beautiful. It was key to her success.

But Malala's success was a threat to the Taliban. They could no longer dismiss her as just a child.

In January 2012, the Sindh government informed us that it would be renaming a girls' secondary school after Malala. We were invited to Karachi by Geo TV. We decided to fly to Karachi—Malala's first time on a plane—as a family, except without Khushal who was at his boarding school in Abbottabad.

While we were in Karachi, a Pakistani journalist from Alaska who was a supporter of Malala's came to the hostel where we were staying and told me of a threat from the Taliban on Malala's life, and that of another female women's rights activist. "Both of them are not good people," the Taliban quote said. "They are working for the West and they are on our target list." More threats were to follow.

This was the worst day of my life so far, the worst. It was the first time I felt an icy fear that Malala could be in danger grip me. That day, somebody was hosting a lunch for us, but I could not eat. I felt so traumatized. I had been prepared for my own death, but this threat to my daughter's life? It was intolerable. I think I must have gone to the bathroom seven times, with a nervous need to pass urine. These absences from the table were so obvious that I had to apologize to my hosts. I told Malala of the threat, but unlike me she was calm.

What should I do? I did not know. When we returned to Mingora from Karachi, I went to the police, and they showed me a file on Malala and how her national and international profile had attracted the attention of the Taliban. They told me she needed guards, but I did not like this idea. I doubted that a guard would keep her safe, as other activists in Swat had been killed despite having guards. I was worried, too, about the other children in the Khushal School.

Instead, I rang a friend, Haider Ali Hamdard, who was a doctor in Abbottabad, for advice. We discussed a famous girls' boarding school there and we decided that it would be wise to move Malala from the Khushal School in Mingora to Abbottabad, which was much more peaceful. We were lucky. The school said it would accept her. I could not afford the fees, but her high profile meant she would be an honorary student. We were working towards her enrollment in January 2013, which was the start of the school year. Then I went to the security authorities and I told them, "I will be shifting Malala to Abbottabad," but they replied, "Well, if you keep a low profile, there is no difference between Swat and Abbottabad. Why shift her there?"

I stopped speaking out myself so that people in Mingora began to think, "Why has he gone so quiet?" We became very selective about what Malala did. I refused to let her accept the offer to become the peace ambassador for the Khyber Pakhtunkhwa government. I told them, "I am sorry, but at the moment she will not be a peace ambassador for anything."

Malala did speak at engagements during 2012, but not as much. I used to say to her, "Please don't say the word 'Taliban.' Just call them 'terrorists' instead."

"Aba," she would say, "they call themselves Taliban. So what should I call them? This is their name. This is their identity."

If I had said to her "Stop campaigning now!" I do not think she would have obeyed. I could have refused to accompany her, but this would have felt like a betrayal of both what Malala herself wanted and our family's values. Her conviction was so strong. She knew her own power by then.

All around us people were scared of the Taliban, and their fear was real and justified. This real fear makes our courage look unreal. For us, because everybody else had fled from the battlefield and only a handful of people were left, it was a reason for us to carry on. We were the only chance left. It sounds crazy, but this is in our DNA.

Still, this year of 2012 in Pakistan was a terrible one for me. I lived in fear constantly. I was no longer a lion on the battlefield. I was jumpy and agitated, not because of the threat to me, but because of the threat to Malala. The Taliban's threats were often empty, I knew that. How many times had there been threats, only for nothing to happen? But I had also lost friends. A large part of me still thought, "Not a child! Never a child!" But I was always looking over my shoulder, far more than in the beginning of 2009, when I could have been taken off in the night and beheaded.

The Taliban attacked Malala on October 9, 2012. The facts of what happened to her have been told many times in the past six years, in newspapers, on televisions all over the world, and in her bestselling book and an award-winning film. In what you have read here, I, too, have tried to relive those days so you can understand how nearly losing her affected not only me but the whole family. But for Malala, the attack on her life is like a myth. She describes it now as just a story. I know that sounds very odd, but she cannot remember anything about the attack or much of the days afterwards. She says, "Aba, when I hear the stories—that there's a girl named Malala who was shot by the Taliban—it's just a story for me. I just don't link it to my life at all. I'm still the same." So this is our second blessing. Our daughter might bear the physical scars of what happened to her, but somehow she has managed to cut herself free from the most distressing elements of her story and soar above them, looking down on the evidence of how she nearly lost her life with a soul unmarked by tragedy and a resolve undiminished. Malala is right. She is the same. She is the same calm, hard-working girl she has always been. She is that same brave bird she was in Mingora, committed and free.

THE WOMEN ARE COMING TO WIN YOU AN HONOR

Malala has said that she knew her life of activism would continue as she was lying in the hospital in Birmingham, even before we got to her bedside: "I was in a kind of puzzle about what other people thought," she told me later. "Did anybody even know I'd been attacked?" One of the nurses brought her a box of get-well cards, containing best wishes sent from Japan, from America, from people six years old to ninety-two. "Wow," she said to the nurse. "So many people supporting me!" The nurse looked astonished. "This is just one box, Malala. We have thousands of cards. We have boxes and boxes and boxes. You are seeing a fraction of it."

"As soon as I started realizing that I did not stand alone in this fight, this is what gave me courage and hope for the future. I have survived for a reason." This is what Malala said to us.

Her life was so nearly taken. The bullet had been so near to her brain. But she had survived. "I will never look back," she said.

Around this time, I had been working on memory tests with her. I had asked her to recite to me some Tapey, old Pashtun poetry that goes back centuries. She told me about one she remembered but that she wanted to change.

She recited the original: "If the men cannot win the battle, O my country, / Then the women will come forth and win you an honor."

"But, Aba," she said, "I would like to change it to "Whether the men are winning or losing the battle, O my country, / The women are coming and the women will win you an honor."

I said to her, "Oh, Malala, what are you saying? You are amazing."

And I cried more tears, but no longer just in sorrow.

THE CATEGORIZATION OF BARACK OBAMA

While Malala was in the hospital, first full-time, then visiting for ongoing treatment, Pekai and I needed somebody to drive us to and from the facility. One day, our driver, Shahid Hussain, who had become our friend, arrived with news of *Time* magazine's 2013 list of the one hundred most influential people in the world. Malala was on the cover, and inside she was ranked number fifteen. President Barack Obama was fifty-one. "I am such a big fan of Malala," our friend told us. "Please, I request you show this report to her. She will be so happy." He gave me his mobile phone to show her. I took the phone and I showed it to Malala. I was so proud of what was on the screen.

She took the phone from me and studied it. And then she put it down. "Well," she said, "I do not believe in such categorization of human beings."

I learn from her every day.

BENAZIR BHUTTO'S SCARF

For us, as Malala's parents, after October 2012 nothing mattered as long as Malala was on this planet. We were just happy that God had given her this second life, that she existed in our lives.

Our house was divided about what might come next. Malala saw her life now with renewed purpose. Pekai, though, was very anxious. As Malala settled into school life in Birmingham, we began the process of writing her book, *I Am Malala,* with Christina Lamb, which after publication required more travel and recounting Malala's story.

I was neutral about whether or not Malala should carry on as a campaigner, but it is hard now to think that she might not have done so. Still, Pekai phoned her eldest brother in Pakistan, the same one who was my teacher and inspiration.

"Tell me," he said to her. "Answer this one question. Have you saved her life or has God saved her life?" Pekai answered, "God has saved her life. I did not." And he said, "If God has saved her, then he has saved her for a reason. You cannot stop her. Don't waste your time, please. You just support her. Let God complete his purpose. You cannot protect her. Do not intervene in God's plan. Just support it and respect it."

It made so much sense. We felt the world needed Malala's voice, so free of blame or hate or jealousy. Love is the most powerful thing human beings can have. Peace and passion can overcome violence. Malala is not aggressive, she is not violent, she is not angry. If ever she is angry, still she is not cruel. She chooses words that fall hard and deep on ears but without ever hurting the listener or the oppressor. This kind of approach is beautiful. It is so powerful. You challenge, but you do not hurt.

You just knock on the door, but you do not break it with stones. You knock on it once, and if there is nothing, then again and again and again. And still you do not break it down with tools. Weapons may bring immediate power, or immediate change, but it is not the long-lasting kind. The long-lasting change is what you stand for, believe in.

Malala began her second life with resilience, patience, and love. Her aim has always been that the people who block her path will join with her in the end. They will be part of her journey because of the peaceful way in which it is traveled.

One day, before the attack, I was asked by an army brigadier, "Would you tell me what Malala has done to make her so popular in Pakistan that everybody is praising her? Tell me why there are newspapers and media all around her."

And I told him the story of the Prophet Abraham (AS). King Namrood wanted him dead and intended to burn him alive. He made a very big fire and put Abraham in the middle. There was a bird in the sky who took water in its beak, and dropped a small drop down on the flames. It did not help, but the bird continued, one drop after another. No drop of water from a small bird's beak would ever be enough, but that bird has become very famous in our stories. It did not give up.

And so I told the army brigadier, "Whether your efforts are small or big, if you have purity of intention and those intentions are in tune with history, then you reach the hearts of people."

I want to tell another story of a man in my own family who has made a change during Malala's life. One of my older cousins was so shocked to see me write Malala's name on the family tree that he made a sort of grimace with his face. It was an undeniable expression of disapproval that a girl should be acknowledged.

But after seeing Malala's pure activism, he changed his mind. His daughters now go to medical school. So my cousin who was once critical of Malala's gender is now her biggest supporter. The pictures of her in the media he once resented? He now shares those pictures himself proudly.

Nine months after the attack, Malala was invited by former UK prime minister Gordon Brown to celebrate her sixteenth birthday by giving an address to the United Nations in New York. This was a deep honor, but we were worried in the beginning. It was a huge pressure and she had been through so much physically. It had not yet been a year since the attack. We thought, "What will happen with this girl? The whole world is looking at her and they have such big expectations. She is just sixteen years old—can she be up to this overwhelming standard?" But then I looked at her strength, and I realized that I could not advise her. I thought, "Zia, God knows that those tiny shoulders can carry the weight."

We did not talk much about it in the run-up. She was so focused on her schoolwork and her homework. But it was getting so close to the date that, in the end, I felt compelled to say, "Jani, there are only ten days remaining." She was so composed, so poised. If it had been me, I would have had my hair standing on end. I'd have been a man in a panic. But Malala never panics. She is calm.

One afternoon, after school, she came to me with a piece of paper covered in writing in pencil. She had drafted her speech during a free period at school. When I read it, I saw the lines "Weakness, fear and hopelessness died. Strength, power, and courage were born. I am the same Malala."

I called out, "Pekai! Pekai! We have our same Malala." Our daughter was more resilient. More powerful. More determined. The power she had was growing greater, not diminishing.

The speech also included these lines: "One child, one teacher, one book, one pen can change the world....Education is the only solution. Education first."

This greater power, this global mission, Pekai and I thought, we take as gifts from God that come with our daughter's life. Malala's status and her responsibility to millions of girls around the world come with her life, celebrated like a child's life with a birthday card.

Everything that was sent to Malala when she was unwell meant so much to us all because it showed the world was with her. One thing, however, was especially important to Jani. Benazir Bhutto has always been Malala's role model. She was a strong woman who received an education and became the first female prime minister of our country, twice. She was also exiled from our country, and ultimately killed for her beliefs. Malala viewed her as a talent lost, a woman smart and strong who was killed for what she believed in. Among the gifts that were sent to Malala were a card and some presents from Benazir Bhutto's children. But also in the package were two of Benazir Bhutto's scarves. When they arrived, Malala lifted the scarves to her face and took in the smell. She was astounded that she was holding them. She was so happy to have them.

It made perfect sense that when she delivered her UN speech she should wear one of these scarves. She chose the white one, and wrapped it around her shoulders, over her dark pink scarf. As Jani walked onto the stage of the UN wearing Bhutto's scarf around her shoulders, I thought of her crouched down by the tap, a small girl scrubbing her own school scarf clean. It had seemed impossible then that she could value any scarf as much as the one she wore as part of her school uniform. But because of her devotion to the cause of education, Malala now had another precious scarf, one she could value just as much.

DON'T KNOW ME AS THE GIRL WHO WAS SHOT

In the run-up to Malala's speech to the UN, there was a small reception for us, hosted by Tina Brown, the British-born, New York–based editor and commentator. Malala was standing in the corner. Somebody gave her a microphone and she started talking. It was a small gathering and I don't think she had intended to speak to the room, especially as the big speech was to come the following day.

"I don't want to be known as the girl who was shot," she said. "I want to be known as the girl who fought."

Once again, I thought, "Oh, Malala, what are you saying?" My tears came. "She is right. She is right." For so long, she had been hearing and reading in the media of "the girl who was shot. The girl who was shot." She was so tired of being that. And so she said, "Don't know me as this thing. Know me as the girl who fought."

A SURPRISE IN CHEMISTRY CLASS

Malala's favorite subject had always been physics but it was in the midst of a chemistry lesson that she found out she'd won the Nobel Peace Prize for 2014.

Since the UN speech in 2013, combined with the publication of *I Am Malala,* her profile had become global. As cofounders of the Malala Fund, we traveled everywhere together, just as we did when we were in Pakistan.

There had been a lot of speculation in 2013 that she would win the Nobel prize. The media in Pakistan seemed to be waiting for this announcement. Malala and I were in America together, campaigning, and I was getting many telephone calls asking, "Have you had the call yet? Usually they call in advance."

A year later, on October 10—one day after the second anniversary of her attack—it did not cross Malala's mind that she would win this honor. A colleague from the Malala Fund was coming to our house to watch the ceremony announcing the winner with me. "Please," Malala said as she left the house for school in her dark green uniform. "It's like 0.0000001 percent that it might be me. Nothing is going to happen. I am going to school!"

We settled on the sofa. I was very excited that, in thirty minutes perhaps, I would receive a call on my phone. No call.

"Well, let's watch it anyway," said my colleague. We put the iPad on the table in front of us and sat there. A door opened on the screen and Thorbjørn Jagland, chairman of the Nobel Committee, entered the assembly and stood behind the podium. The winners were announced: Kailash Satyarthi and Malala Yousafzai.

I jumped! I jumped high off the sofa and I hugged my colleague. Toor Pekai joined us. It was an unforgettable moment. It was such recognition at such a young age. For me, being the father of a seventeen-year-old girl who was going to be a Nobel laureate, this was incredible. It doesn't happen in dreams. It is beyond dreams. Beyond any dreams I had when I wanted to break to pieces the scissors of our society that would have cut her wings.

When the deputy head of the school knocked on the door of the chemistry class and said she'd like to take Malala to see the headmistress, Malala instinctively thought, "Oh, dear, what's the problem?" It was the headmistress who broke the good news to her.

Later, Malala gave a speech to the whole of Edgbaston High School for Girls. It was the only time in her school career that she allowed herself to be "Malala" the activist rather than just an ordinary schoolgirl. The teachers were crying. The students were crying. But Malala did not cry, not with them and not with us later on.

She did not come home after the announcement. Of course not! She finished her school day, and when she arrived back home, we hugged. And Toor Pekai and I cried.

For me as a father, I had a few feelings about this prize. This prize changed Malala into "the teenager who won the Nobel."

A few months after that day, I went to Winnipeg to make a speech and I met a small child, the son of my cousin. I crouched beside him and said, "So you know Malala?"

"Yes, I know her," the boy said. "She is the girl who got the Nobel Peace Prize."

"Yes, that is right," I said. And the child must surely have thought, "Who is this strange man, crying at my simple answer?"

It was such a wonderful thing to happen for her campaign. As Malala herself said, "I was walking, and now the Nobel is a bike to my destiny."

Malala was not interested in any personal glory. "This award is for the issue, Aba," she said. "It will help us raise the issue globally and bring more attention to our campaign for girls' education." And she is right. It has had a great impact on Malala's success as a campaigner and fund-raiser for the Malala Fund. More and more people are talking about the importance of education for all girls and especially those children who are growing up in parts of the world where there is conflict.

Sometimes I imagine what her life would have been like without the Talibanization of our home, if we had all been able to stay in Pakistan. I really believe that she would have been the same amazing girl, playing a central role in public life, not globally yet but definitely in Pakistan. She was flourishing in peacetime. In another life, at the age of twenty, Malala would perhaps be studying now at Lahore University of Management Sciences (LUMS). She would not have achieved the Nobel Peace Prize in this alternative life. She probably would not have had anywhere near half the accolades and prizes that fill our home, but she would still have been Malala.

CONKERS IN EDGBASTON

For six years now, we have lived in Edgbaston, a leafy area of Birmingham where the streets are full of the kinds of trees that Pekai and I had only ever seen at the very top of the mountains in Shangla and Swat. In the flat fields where we grew up, we were used to playing in the orchards, the branches of the various trees hanging with every kind of fruit. We had trees thick with apples and peaches and pears, oranges and persimmons, the last a delicious fruit from a tree that is quite common in

Japan. It was normal for us to live among these fruits. But other trees, such as chestnuts and oaks, conifers and pines, were only ever seen on treks to the top of the mountain, such as the time I climbed up the mountain with my mother to see the saint for my stammering.

From the very beginning of our new life in the UK, I would marvel at being able to walk to the shops passing by the trunks of the chestnut trees and the oaks. Seeing their branches and their leaves made me feel like I was back home. For Pekai, these trees were her friends. Sometimes, she would talk to them in Pashto: "Oh, dear tree, you were there with us in Shangla and in Swat. Who has brought you over here with us?"

In winter, there is always a sea of shiny brown conkers (horse chestnuts) just like there was on the mountaintops in Shangla. We call the trees *jawaz*. In Pakistan, we do not attach conkers to strings the way children do in the UK, but we use them as natural marbles. In my childhood, I remember my sisters creating toy houses, a shiny conker representing a buffalo or a cow in the pasture. For Pekai, she remembers how these conkers were used by her mother's friends, their seeds extracted to create a kind of medicine for bone or joint pain.

In Edgbaston, October is the prime time for conkers. We never tired of seeing them lying on the ground.

This year, their fall coincided with us taking Malala to Oxford to begin her degree. I knew I would miss her, but I allowed my tears to fall only once, the night she left, when I handed her a bag of dried fruit as I used to do when she was studying for her A levels.

I have learned that I must not be possessive, that as my children grow older I must let go. The more Malala is independent, the more she is living on her own, the more she grows into a fully fledged human being, the more rewarding my love for her is. Because seeing her live a life based on her decisions alone is all I have ever wanted. This is a reward for me.

These days, it is rare that Malala is in Edgbaston. She lives almost all of the time in Oxford. She has made so many friends there. We have visited her four or five times so far and each time I meet her friends I feel so happy that my daughter is surrounded by people who love her. For these new friends, Malala is not a Nobel laureate but just a young woman, a fellow undergraduate who is a member of international societies, debating societies, and even the cricket club.

It has been much easier for her than it was when she started in Edgbaston High School because of the simple fact that she joined Lady Margaret Hall at the same time as everybody else. She is an ordinary student like everybody else.

When Jani got to Oxford, everything went so well apart from one thing: there were spiders in her room. She telephoned me and said, "Aba, I do not like them there." Atal is absolutely terrified of spiders. Malala does not have this phobia, but still, she is not comfortable with them in her room. I wanted to help. When I shared my dilemma with our local pharmacist, she said to me, "I advise you to send her some fresh conkers to place in the corners of the room. Spiders do not like them."

The *jawaz* of Edgbaston! That afternoon, I put on my long coat and I walked around the sidewalks that had once felt so strange. The conkers were all around my feet and I filled my pockets with them until they bulged out of each side. The following day, I went to the post office and I filled an envelope with the conkers and a note telling Malala to put them in the corners of the room. The next time Malala rang, she said, "Aba, I think the spiders might have gone!"

Your children might not need you in obvious ways, but as a parent it is nice to know you still have your uses.

FAMILIAR ADVICE

I like telephoning Malala for advice. Should I tweet this particular political thought? What should I do if I am having difficulty in expressing an idea? How do I get my iPhone to do this or that particular function? And she guides me. "Aba, do this, do that, do this." She has always guided me. As a seven-year-old girl, she would say to me when I asked her opinion about the progress of the Khushal School, "Aba, I think it is sort of crawling along like an ant."

Now she often says to me about my own capabilities, "Aba, you *can* learn these things yourself, but you don't believe in yourself. You think you can't learn. But if you pay a bit more attention to these things, then you will learn how to do them. Please don't automatically think that these things are not for you."

Malala often travels without me now, accompanied by people from the Malala Fund instead. We have traveled all over the world together as part of our campaign for girls' education, but she no longer needs me by her side. The way she puts it is that you do not wake up one morning and think, "I no longer want this..." or "I'm ready for that now..." but that it is a gradual process where you feel your way towards something new. I suppose this is called growing up.

When baby birds are born, they do not know how to fly. They have an instinct for it, but no practice, so they watch the mother bird, who leaves the nest often, flying backwards and forwards dropping food into their beaks. The baby bird begins to feel a bit bolder, and seeing this, the parent bird moves farther away so that the chick is encouraged to come out onto the branch seeking its food. The baby bird often falls to the ground with a thump when it tries to lift its wings, but the mother bird does not panic. The mother flies again and again, and gradually its baby learns to copy. Even when the little bird does this once or twice, it is not easy or instant. No. The chick has to train the muscles in its wings so that it can flap with more strength. And all the time, the mother bird is watching, reinforcing the message of this wing flapping by her own flight. And then, one day, the baby bird raises itself up off the branch, and it flaps its wings so hard that it is effortlessly carried high into the air. This is the moment it realizes that it no longer needs its mother or any other bird to bring it food or to offer it protection. It is the moment when it realizes that it can fly away to wherever it wants. The mother bird never stops this from happening. She would be a very poor mother bird if she did.

Malala did not want to travel alone to the United Nations in New York when she was sixteen. She did not want to travel to the refugee camps in Syria for her eighteenth birthday without me. But she is twenty-one now. In February, while she was at Oxford, she left for a ten-day trip. She went to the World Economic Forum in Davos and she went to Jordan, where she had a press conference with Tim Cook, the CEO of Apple and a Malala Fund donor. Mostly we leave her to manage her Malala Fund schedule, but her position means that she has many more demands on her time than an ordinary twenty-one-year-old. Only when we see signs of the workload becoming too much do we step in and suggest, "No more travel for a while. You must concentrate on being young."

I feel proud that there is this kind of human being on our earth, whose life is about others. I feel proud of this young woman called Malala, who tries to teach the world that love is all about others, that it is not all about you. I feel proud that this young woman called Malala has learned to love herself and value herself but places herself in the bigger perspective of the world, one that must provide twelve years of quality education to girls globally. And I feel proud, too, that this young woman called Malala is busy with her own education at Oxford, with going to parties, buying clothes, and counting her steps on her Fitbit.

And only after all these thoughts do I allow myself to feel proud that this young woman called Malala was also that baby who lay in our secondhand cradle. I am so proud that Malala is my daughter.

Epilogue

GOING HOME

F OR YEARS, IN my dreams I have returned to Pakistan, to Swat and to Shangla. And in the morning, I have woken up to find myself thousands of miles from home. For such a long time, Toor Pekai and I and Malala have longed to have those dreams come true.

But for us, for Toor Pekai and me, since the attempt on Malala's life, everything has been about safety, about safeguarding her life.

It was Malala herself who could no longer bear not returning to Pakistan. "I left my home, I left my country, and it was not my choice," she said. "I went to school that morning and I never came back. I left my country in an induced coma."

I will confess that although I am so happy for Malala to travel all over the world without us, I was nervous about her returning to Pakistan.

"Please, Jani, let us just wait one more year." Toor Pekai was also hesitant initially, and Khushal was frightened. For weeks he either had terrible nightmares or could not sleep at all. I would hear him moving about the house in the night, restless and anxious.

But Malala meant to go. "If we all don't go back to Pakistan together," she told us, "I will go on my own. I have to go." And so I said, "We are coming."

I cannot put into words how I felt when our plane touched down in Pakistan and we stepped onto the ground in Islamabad. I think not even poets have invented words for something like this. Words cannot do justice to such intensity of feeling. When words fail, smiles and tears come, and that expresses all that is inside you.

Malala does not often cry. Since her attack, I have seen her cry only three times. The first was when we finally arrived at the hospital in the UK after a ten-day separation and she saw us by her bedside. The second time was on her eighteenth birthday, when we saw the refugees crossing the border from Syria to Jordan, and the third time was when she was listening to a mother talking about how her son had been badly wounded by the Taliban shooting in the army public school. But during her first official engagement in Pakistan, in front of three hundred people, she could not stop crying. The whole auditorium was crying. The whole world saw Malala crying because her tears were an expression of her happiness.

"This is the happiest day of my life," she said.

When Malala was shot and fighting for her life, her body was lifted in a helicopter from a helipad in Mingora. As the helicopter carried us over the valley to the hospital in Peshawar, I sat beside her as she was on the stretcher vomiting blood. We had left Pekai below, standing there with her arms aloft, her scarf in her hands above her head, a direct appeal to God to bring back her daughter safely. I had seen nothing outside the helicopter then, no air, no land, because then I was with Malala, looking at her body, trying to gauge how she was responding to the trauma, how she was struggling to hang on to her life.

This time, we five were together in the helicopter, healthy and safe, as it flew back over the same mountains to that same helipad in Mingora from where Malala began her journey away from her homeland. It felt like a triumph. We looked down on the fields and mountains and lakes and dams and familiar scenes of our beautiful Swat, the place that has shaped all that we are. It was like a gift from God, truly God's gift to our family.

When we got off the helicopter, on that helipad where I had once thought death was claiming my child, the five of us huddled together. We held one another so tightly. Toor Pekai and I could not stop our tears. The helipad is only a couple of minutes from our old house in Mingora. Malala had state-level security surrounding her, which the army was facilitating. We went to our house. When we reached its white walls and its gated courtyard, I fell to the floor and put my hands on the soil. I had to touch the soil of the land, I had to have it on my palms. I kissed that soil. I kissed it as when you might greet a beloved, a mother, after a long, long time. You just want to hug that precious thing close to your body.

Malala and the boys ran to the rooms that had once been theirs. Malala saw the designs on the wall she had made when she was a child, and she saw the trophies that she had won as part of the education she had tried to save.

*   *   *

When we left Mingora, the helicopter took us to Swat Cadet College, a school run by the army, at the bottom of the mountains. A red carpet waited for Malala, and she walked across it to the place where we were given lunch. On the way back to the helicopter, in the distance we saw a big crowd of army soldiers, lined up with their vehicles. As we walked past them, Malala waved and the soldiers in their uniforms took off their caps in salute to her, a sign of their deepest respect for her. This was one of the beautiful highlights of our Pakistan tour.

Malala's very presence in Pakistan was a change for our country. It symbolized change. She did not even have to speak because her physical presence itself was the embodiment of peace and education.

We held two lunches for our family and friends from Shangla and Swat, almost all of whom we had not seen since we left suddenly in 2012. We were expecting one hundred people from Shangla, but more than three hundred traveled to the hotel in order to meet Malala and see us. It was an eight-hour drive. My second mother was among this group. I had not seen her for six years, and when she was wheeled through the door in her wheelchair, it was such a moving sight. I felt a rush of love for her, and it suddenly occurred to me that I wanted to present her with some flowers, as a sign of my deep affection. But I had no flowers. When I looked around, however, I saw that there was a hotel display. It was a white arrangement, and I would have preferred colored flowers, but even so, I grabbed several of the stems and I knelt down beside my mother and gave her the flowers and told her I loved her. It felt a bit like I had stolen these flowers, but the hotel was very kind and generous about my taking them. I think perhaps

I was overcome by a kind of madness. The second day, we were again expecting around one hundred people from Swat, but again more than three hundred arrived. In these crowds, there were families of three generations, from babies to old men in their nineties. It brought me such happiness to see everybody sitting together in the same room, celebrating our journey back home. Malala moved about the tables, ensuring that everybody felt they had been personally welcomed by her.

When Malala was in the presence of Prime Minister Shahid Khaqan Abbasi, he stood four times for her as she passed him to go to the stage to deliver her speech. "Malala," he said, "you are no longer an ordinary citizen of Pakistan. You are the most famous Pakistani woman in the world."

"The bad days are gone," I thought. "Jani is back in her country and the people are supportive. She will carry on her campaign for every girl in every village, in every city, and in every country, for the 130 million girls who do not go to school."

And one day, we might all be able to finally come home.

Acknowledgments

The great Urdu poet Saleem Kausar has a beautiful verse that reads: سر آئینہ مرا عکس ہے پس آئینہ کوئی اور ہے. ("There is my reflection in front of the mirror, but there is another [are many] behind the mirror.")

Although this book has my name on it, this verse speaks for all the people, family and friends, who helped bring it to life.

Writing it has been a journey for me, as it has been for many others, and I believe myself to be very lucky to have found Louise Carpenter as my coauthor. Therefore, my first and foremost gratitude goes to her. This has been an intellectually challenging and emotionally charged journey. With Louise being an amazing listener and a wonderful writer, this journey was an incredibly enriching experience. She laughed, cried, and smiled with me while I was sharing my stories and experiences. She put her heart and soul into articulating my story in the best possible way. Thank you, Louise, for making this book a reality with me.

I may be the narrator of this book, but I couldn't have completed it without my better half, my great friend and companion, my wife, Toor Pekai. Throughout this process, sitting with Louise in our sessions, sometimes I would glimpse a memory without fully recollecting it. I would call out "TOOR PEKAI!" and she would come running. Having an elephant's memory, she provided full details of the stories I wanted to tell. Thank you, Toor Pekai, for being generous and passionate in your contributions and for being there for me every single time I needed you in my life.

The world rightly knows me as Malala's proud father. But I am also blessed in being the father of my two amazing sons, Khushal Khan and Atal Khan. Both of them are unique and special in their own way. This book is a story of father and sons, too. Thank you, Khushal and Atal, for being honest in your input.

Malala asked me for a long time to write a book. As her book *I Am Malala* has many of the stories of our family, in this book she wanted me to give my unique perspective. She helped me in setting the vision of this book, and in spite of her very busy schedule at Oxford, she shared her part of the story and penned the foreword. Thank you, my dear Jani, for being my strength and for standing with me from your childhood to this very day, every day!

Apart from my family, I am thankful to Darnell Strom and Jamie Joseph, who were keen to motivate me. Adam Grant, the coauthor of *Option B,* inspired me so much when he wrote with words of encouragement. Thank you, Adam, for your kind words.

My friend and my son Khushal's mentor Simon Sinek deserves my gratitude, too. In just one session, he resolved my dilemma about the title and suggested *Let Her Fly,* which resonated with me and all those involved. Thank you, Simon, for your wisdom and vision.

Our family has been very lucky to have had great people around us since we moved to the UK. One of these is Karolina Sutton, a wonderful woman whose professional honesty has always impressed me. She is a sincere family friend whom we trust very much. Thank you, Karolina, for supporting our literary work.

I am very thankful to Judy Clain from Little, Brown for her personal interest in the book and for her constant encouragement, and for strictness on the deadlines. She has all the great qualities an editor should have. Thank you, Judy; much respect.

I am also immensely grateful to Maria Qanita, our family friend and coordinator, who supported this project in so many ways, from managing my itinerary to engaging in intellectual discussions. Eason Jordan, a great family friend, was quick to help when I requested family photographs. Eason, thank you. As I have often said, "Where there is Eason, there is a way." Thank you to Qasim Swati and Tom Payne for their poetic translations of my poems, which add more value to the book. And finally, thank you to Usman Ali, who is like an adopted brother to me and has helped our family so much over the years.

I hope this book is an enriching and joyful experience for all the readers and conveys the love, warmth, and affection that my friends and family hold for one another.

In gratitude, Ziauddin Yousafzai

There are many people who helped me along the way with their insights and hospitality: Maryam Khalique, Hai Kakar, Dr. Fiona Reynolds and her husband, Adrian Bullock, and Toor Pekai's friend and teacher Janet Culley-Tucker. I am also grateful to the extended Yousafzai family in Pakistan who gave their various help and permission to use their stories. Usman Bin Jan provided the delicious food. I love an English cup of tea, but I concede that *dhood patti* is the best. Samina Nawaz was such a happy presence.

I would like to thank the Yousafzai family. Toor Pekai, for tolerating my long days with Ziauddin and trusting me with her story, so important in its own right; Khushal and Atal, for being honest about difficult periods in their lives while also making me laugh; and Malala, for finding the time in an insane schedule to talk to me.

Thank you to my agent, Karolina Sutton, for keeping us on the right road; Judy Clain, who guided me with a mixture of clarity and trust; Betsy Uhrig, a respectful and diligent production editor; and Jamie Joseph, my British editor, for strong support. I could not have met my deadline without Sophie Swietochowski, who accurately transcribed hours of conversations.

The literary judgment and love of my husband, Tom Payne, are invaluable, and my dear children have been patient and involved throughout.

Above all, I would like to thank Ziauddin. It has been hard work but also such tremendous fun. There is no other word for it. We laughed and very often we cried. I feel privileged to have helped tell this story of bravery and goodness. And in doing so, I feel I have made a friend for life.

Louise Carpenter

About the Authors

Ziauddin Yousafzai is an educational activist, a human rights campaigner, and a teacher. He hails from Pakistan's Swat Valley, where, at great personal risk in an atmosphere of fear and violence, he stood up and peacefully resisted the Taliban's efforts to shut down schools and limit personal freedoms. He continued his campaign for education after moving to the United Kingdom and, as the cofounder of the Malala Fund with his daughter, Malala, he is building a movement of support for twelve years of girls' education worldwide. He has been conferred with an honorary doctorate of law by the Wilfrid Laurier University of Canada, and he serves as the global ambassador for the Women in Public Service Project, on the leadership council of the Global Women's Institute (GWI) of the George Washington University, and as the United Nations Special Advisor on Global Education.

Louise Carpenter is a British writer working primarily for the Saturday *Times Magazine*. Her work has also been published in many other publications, including *Granta, The Guardian, The Telegraph,* and *Vogue,* and has been syndicated worldwide. She is the author of two nonfiction books and lives in Somerset, England, with her family.